WE RISE

JASMINE

POOLE

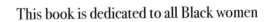

This book is dedicated to all Black women

Contents

1

Struggle & Strength

She stands in the doorway of America as blood mixed with sweat drips from her head to her feet, Prime Girl on the auction block labeled as livestock, after having worked sunup to sundown in the cotton fields from 1619 to 1856. When have Black women ever been "free" from struggle, says the blisters on her hands from picking cotton for four hundred years to her bruised knees from scrubbing floors through the mid 1900's? She has been raped, beaten, and suffocated with the grip of poverty. The Black man is absent; her children are hungry. Doing the best she can to provide. Her tears splash down on her dreams she buried as a little girl when she found out that equal opportunity never existed for her. Now, she's left in the doorway of America looking at the land of opportunity from the outside.

Peaceful Defiance

<u>MELANIN</u>

"Children, who made your skin White? Was it not God? Who made mine Black? Was it not the same God? Am I to blame, therefore, because my skin is Black?" Sojourner Truth (Spinale, 1999)

Complexion has been a historical, generational, ancestral tool to divide and separate us as Black women. Colorism is a form of internalized racism. The way we invalidate ourselves and sometimes each other as Black women is by comparing our shade to our worth. Our history during the years of slavery is a prime example of this. The lightest Black women during slavery were in the "big house", which in those days stood for the White master's house, while the darker skin women worked out in the field. The famous politician Barbara Jordan was born in 1936, and the

2

first words her father said when she was born was, "Why is she so dark?" (McNair, 2000) For so long, the past generations have forced Black women to stay silent about colorism and the effect it has had on our people. It has been embedded in our cellular memory to separate ourselves based on our skin tones. We must eliminate the idea that our pigment as Black women has to look a certain way to be acceptable in society. Our ancestors were brainwashed into believing dark skin was ugly and that people with light skin were the only ones beautiful. During slavery, it was a known fact that the darker women would be beaten profusely, impregnated inhumanly, and sold faster than slaves with lighter skin. The Black women closest to White were treated with higher status and received more recognition. The slave auctioneers would say, "You're not buying her for her brains but for her muscles, and you can see she's a big, strapping girl who can work hard and won't give nobody trouble." (Lester, 2005)

Throughout American history, African Americans have had to deal with discriminatory practices. One of which is known as the "Brown Paper Bag Test''. During the 20th century, the "Brown Paper Bag Test" became extremely well known throughout the African-American community. This test was meant to compare an individual's skin tone to the color of a brown paper bag. This test was originally used to decide what privileges certain people of color would be allowed. This test would be later included in churches, schools, and other organizations such as sororities and fraternities. Melanin tones went by different titles based on your Blackness. An example of this is the label *"quadroons"*, which meant that you were ¼ Black, or *"octoroons" which* represented being ⅛ Black. These were all ways to categorize the African American race. As time progressed, so did the lens in which African Americans viewed themselves. Some say the Blacker the berry, the sweeter the juice. I say the darker the flesh then the deeper the roots." (Tupac Shakur, 1993)

3

WE RISE

The production of light skinned mixed children came from slave masters who raped the lighter skin Black women. The lighter your skin, the more privileges you were given. The babies who were born were "mixed", interracial, which continued the color division cycle that took place generation after generation on the plantations. Although we are in the twenty-first century, not much has been shifted in the thought process. We as Black women have been cultured to compare and not connect. Race is subjective to lighter skin Black women, they are bombarded with, "What are you mixed with?" or "You're not Black enough". So, many biracial Black women live their entire life being called light bright, yellow, White, Black girl or even half and half. These are all the damaging titles millions of beautiful biracial women of color are faced with throughout their entire lives.

Medically, there have been multiple ways to change one's skin, including bleaching cream for lightening or tanning for darkening. Many countries in the western hemisphere, especially common in many parts of Nigeria, Black women bleach their skin with hydroquinone. Hydroquinone is a form of a bleaching cream to lighten the pigmentation in the skin. Hydroquinone, just like many other bleaching creams created, has been found to cause skin cancer. Still, it's a multi-million-dollar business swept off the shelves daily by women of color all around the world. In today's society on social media, there are examples of complexion labels, people say, #TeamDarkSkin or #TeamLightSkin. These seemingly harmless hash tags are just the modern "Brown Paper Bag Test" just another way to build walls of colorism.

"Walking into any room, usually as the only Black woman, I knew that I had this superpower of being able to feel both invisible and hyper-visible at the same time."
Kendeil Dorvilier

ABUSE

"Since we all came from a woman, got our name from a woman and our game from a woman. I wonder why we take from our women, why we rape our women, do we hate our women? I think it's time to kill for our women, time to heal our women, be real to our women." (Tupac Shakur, 1993)

Many times, domestic violence is silenced in the Black community. Historically, the Black woman has been conditioned to protect the Black man at all costs, even if that means sacrificing oneself. Generation after generation of Black women have been stuck in unhealthy toxic abusive relationships. Whether it is financial, physical, emotional, verbal, or sexual abuse, we have been told to be strong and stick it out. We are even told, "Maybe it's something you did to make him angry." Every day, thousands of Black women find themselves tied down by abuse. "One out of every five Black women is a victim of sexual abuse." (Black Women & Sexual Violence, 2020) Victims constantly battle with leaving or staying. They have questions like, "If he is the breadwinner how will the bills get paid if I leave him?" "I don't want my kids to grow up without their dad." "I have to struggle in silence for the sake of my children." The Black community tends to normalize domestic violence.

Not all abuse results in Black eyes or swollen lips. More often than not, abuse scars the victim internally. Abusers are not clear to the human eye at the start of many relationships. Nevertheless, time has a way of revealing a person's truth. Verbal abuse does in fact exist, "And when he tells you you ain't nuttin' don't believe him, and if he can't learn to love you, you should leave him." (Tupac Shakur, 1993) Until we address the violence in every part of our lives as Black women, our scars will not truly heal. If we don't start now every generation of Black women to come will continue to hand over the torch of trauma.

If we as a community want to change, we must challenge the bystanders who witness the abuse. Educating yourself on the red flags of abuse will help heal thousands of Black women now and forever. To break the chains of abuse that have been wrapped around Black women since before slavery, we must report once we are aware. "Over 18% of Black women will be sexually assaulted in their lifetime." (Black Women & Sexual Violence, 2020) The abuse epidemic has always existed in the Black community. "I thought that when a man takes the time to argue with you, that it means he is passionate and devoted to the relationship. The second way I just knew he was the love of my life was because we were both jealous and insecure. Again, I just knew that if he didn't want me around any guys but him, it just meant he loved me and wanted all of my attention." (Contributing Writer Gaskins, 2020) Black women stop being comfortable being uncomfortable.

"When someone shows you who they are, believe them the first time."

Maya Angelou

Fire to the Furnace

by Pebbles D. Poole

For as long as I can remember, my life has never been my choice. From an early age my innocence was taken from me, which caused my life to shift down a road of abundant fear. When most people think back on their childhood, the memories are some of the fondest moments of their lives. Unlike most people, I can't relate to the stereotypical childhood for a young girl. Things like extra-curricular activities, after-school social events, or just doing my homework, never existed for me. I was one of four children; my mother was a military wife, and my stepfather was active duty in the army. I was a *"sibling mother"* who had to cook, clean, and provide care for my younger siblings every day. There were no days off and no going outside to hang out with friends. A normal day meant waking up at the crack of dawn and 5:00 a.m. cooking breakfast for the entire family, while getting myself and my younger siblings all packed and ready for school. Sometimes before going to school, I had to drive my mother to work; she was never the driving type because she had a tremendous fear of being behind the wheel. Occasionally, I would get picked up by my stepfather, who was my abuser. Prior to anyone arriving home from school or work to witness the sexual abuse taking place on occasion was one of the most stripping feelings. I was robbed of my childhood innocence.

I knew I needed to escape, but the big sister inside of me knew that I had to protect my younger sister. When her eyes looked up at me, I instantly saw an infant I needed to save from the horrific pain I had to endure. At that moment, I found the strength to tell my mother what had been happening to me. Although this fear of shame and embarrassment made me feel guilty, scared and dirty, I knew I had to tell my mother.

I took a walk before I ran. On February 13, 1988 I took a walk with my mother to tell her about the abuse that had been happening to me. It was around eleven o'clock at night, very dark. I looked up in the sky, took a big breath of relief, and said "Dad's been touching me". Instantly, we stood there, and she cried and said, "This happened to me too as a girl." Right after this moment, she frantically began scrambling for cover-ups to patch my wounds inside. She began by saying "Where are we going to live; we will become homeless if he goes to jail." We walked back towards the house, and she came out and uttered "Do you think you can live with him?" At that moment I felt I had to say yes, so I went back in the house and went back to being the "*sibling mother*" and victim.

As the days and weeks passed, there I was again waking up at 5:00 a.m. getting my siblings ready for school, juggling chores and remaining in this dark place inside. In the back of my young mind, I constantly wondered, "Why did I even decide to open up and tell my mom what had been going on?" I truly believed that by telling her it would put an end to this distress and victimization. Instead, it just flipped the switch inside me to stop walking, and instead just take off running.

Time passed and when I looked up, it was my senior year in high school. This was one of the best times of my life because, not only was I able to have a snip of my freedom, but I also felt safe knowing my stepfather was deployed for the entire year. I was able to finally be a teenager and not the *"sibling mother"* I had always been. My siblings were all grown up and doing their own thing. I spent time hanging out with friends, enjoying extracurricular activities such as track and field and cheerleading, and spending time with my boyfriend.

Now it's almost the end of my senior year, and I begin to feel the clock ticking. Anxiety filled me up inside, and I struggled with the fear of having to live with the abuser again. Rushing to enroll in college, and my dreams of packing up into a U-Haul truck and moving into a college long far away waving my parents goodbye, was shattered after my parents made clear their disapproval of me going far away to school. So, I stayed local and attended Trenton State College, then transferring to Burlington County College soon after. Still running and fighting the inner pain, I continued to stride forward running. Then my running came to a screeching halt when I became pregnant with me and my high school sweetheart's first child. He was enlisting into the military, and I knew that this would be the perfect opportunity to start a new life and escape the dark shadows that my home life had suffocated me with for so long.

Twenty-year-old mother and military wife living in Germany cut off from the world you've always known. *I thought I finished the long race I had always been running, but little did I know that was just the warmup.* The small petite 120 lb. coke bottle shape, youthful me was gone. There I was 270 lbs. gasping for air running from being married to a man with a mental illness. Struggling to make ends meet still living in Germany, my nine-month-old daughter and I wake up in the middle of the night to military police (MP) banging on our door. Later, having found out that my husband had beaten and robbed a German citizen for money in order to buy formula for our baby. Within that tour of duty, he endured three court marshals, which eventually removed him from the military and labeled him a felon. That took me back to square one, having to move back into my parents' house now with a baby girl and a husband who was dealing with substance abuse and was later diagnosed with bipolar disorder.

The first words that I uttered to my stepfather after my return home were, "If you ever touch her, I will kill you." He looked at me with a face of fear and suspense. At that moment, I knew he knew I was different. I was still running but not broken, not faint. Months passed by, and now by this time, my small little family had landed a small home of our own in Tennessee, with my parents not far away. Soon, we found out the tragic news that my husband's father was dying with a terminal illness from the military (Agent Orange). Just finding out I was pregnant again with our second child, my husband was torn with having to choose to go to New Jersey and be by his father's side in these last moments or be by his wife's side before the new baby was born. My husband chose to drive to New Jersey and be with his father during this time. A few weeks after he left for New Jersey, I was in a horrific car accident in Tennessee while pregnant; I was taken by helicopter to the nearest trauma hospital.

The doctors said my water was leaking and that they were gonna have to run tests, the physician said to me "Your baby will have cognitive delays, reproduction issues; ask your family to pray because we will have to deliver her today because your sack has been ruptured." On September 7, 1994 at 6:00 a.m. in Nashville Tennessee, at age 25 and all alone, I gave birth to a premature 6 lb. baby girl, only twenty-six days before just having gotten the news that my father-in-law passed away. Six weeks later, my husband, kids and I packed up and relocated to New Jersey for a new start. At this moment, the fire began to spark, and my husband's substance abuse worsened due to the trauma of losing his father. We were now living at his mother's house with our two daughters at the time.

One Sunday he drove to church separately and had a manic attack causing him to attempt to kill himself by crashing into a telephone pole. Weeks passed, and my husband, still battling his manic rage, tried drowning me stating I needed to be baptized. Days passed; I stood on the stoop holding our five-month-old premature baby girl, and my husband asked to hold her, seeming calm. I allowed him to hold her at that moment, not knowing his manic state. Then as he held her in his arms he said, "Do you believe in God, and if so, do you think he would protect her from danger if I threw her in the air?" And then, he did just that. My five-month-old baby was thrown in the air and landed on the sidewalk concrete. I tried to push my way to save her, but he stopped me from doing so. Then my brother-in-law came to push him away and get the baby off the ground. We called 911. My baby and I went to the emergency room; she was okay by the grace of God.

My husband was admitted into the psychiatric ward for the first of many times. I knew nothing of what was soon to be revealed. After a few months, he was released, and I forced myself to become educated on what truly mental illness meant. I decided to stay and not continue to run for my children's sake. After seeking Christ, we were able to finally enjoy a healthy happy marriage, until our son whose name means "God with us". After he was born, our happy life came to another screeching halt. The bipolar illness my husband faced reached another level, causing us to almost lose our home and him becoming unemployed due to the self-medicating substance abuse. Here I was in my mid-thirties now and ecstatic about a new baby, a son. This chapter of my life was joy mixed with fear to provide which caused me to take on three or more jobs just to provide for our family. I knew nothing about self-care or self-worth. I always knew my husband loved me no matter how much weight I gained or how unattractive I appeared. He had the biggest heart

11

in spite of the demons he had to endure. I was still running from all of the pain that other people's choices dragged me through.

Years passed, dragging through the final lap of running. It began with waking up to the blaze in the kitchen. Running up the steps at 2:00 a.m. to the alarming smoke detectors, I found my husband passed out drunk with a pot of oil on fire; two out of my three children ran out the house barefoot into the bitterly cold snow. My teenage daughter grabbed her young brother and carried him out the house to safety. My instincts were to first make sure my children were safe and then put out the fire, having had no house phone or cell phones to call for help. I got a bag of flour and doused the fire. This entire time, my husband was still passed out on the floor. *This was when I knew I had run from the fire to the furnace.*

There was no longer anywhere else to run. My house became a maze of destruction, confusion, distress, and fear of the unknown. The final night of our traditional family under one roof ended on December 26, 2012. Walls were plastered with food and bottles of alcohol were piled on the floor, Walls were spray painted with threats and psychotic codes. I was attacked with hateful words and belittling actions, having had smoke blown in my face, pushed down flights of steps, all of my clothes piled up and drenched in bleach, and interior house paint buckets poured on my clothes and furniture. My children had to live with hearing the verbal and emotional abuse. I promised myself I would protect them from anyone, including their father. It was at this moment on December 26, 2012 when my husband picked up our Christmas tree and threw it across the living room, having knocked down my daughter. My legs locked and I was frozen in disbelief, tears filled my eyes, not able to run anymore and hit the shattered Christmas bulbs on the floor. That was the last day of running.

At this point, I was able to find myself. By doing that, I had to put myself first, so I began to learn self-care. My outlook on life became renewed. I always trusted in Jesus and I knew better days would come. No longer was I running from my past, but instead, my children and I had peace in our home. My husband and I separated, but he never went too far; he still remained a part of our lives. Mental illness affects many of our families in the Black community. It is how we educate ourselves rather than calling the person or family member crazy or deranged. My life has been a true testament about how running from the fire to the furnace can cause so much pain. I have been blessed to endure the race my life has taken me on, being a mother of three beautiful young adults and grandmother to two beautiful grandchildren and being a role model in my community.

Having already run that race, I don't want my daughters or any other Black women to run the same race. My journey during this race has had many tears, hurt, harm and danger. Let my life serve as an example of why you shouldn't run. Seek God first and educate yourself on the help that is available for various stages of abuse. Don't STOP telling someone if the first person doesn't help. Know your worth, DON'T RUN!

END

Abuse Red Flags

- Deep silence when a particular person is around
- A change in appetite, weight loss, weight gain
- Embarrassing or putting you down
- Controlling you from seeing your family or friends
- Blaming you for the abuse
- Preventing you from attending work or school
- Unexplained bruises, burns, welts, cuts
- Suicide attempts or other self-harm
- Intimidating you with knives, guns or other weapons

ABANDONMENT

"The most unprotected women in America is the Black women." Malcolm X
This Malcolm X quote is a spine-chilling reality for the majority of Black women. Black women who have dealt with abandonment often never want to be alone because it will force them to confront the intertwined issues within themselves that they might have tried tucking away. Since American slavery took place, Black men and women have yet to fully address and unlearn self-hate, "She was considered less than a woman. She was a cross between a whore and a workhorse. Black men internalized the White man's opinion of Black women. And, if you ask me, a lot of us still act like we're back on the plantation with massa pulling the strings." (Assata Shakur, 1987)

One of the most common examples of traumatic triggers of abandonment is the death of a loved one. Although Black women are some of the most resilient independent humans on earth, do we deserve to be continuously abandoned? Over time, the Black woman has been left in the shadows to be the man and the woman of the household. The vastly growing issue of the abandoned Black woman oftentimes

14

starts with the Black girl or Black boy. The seemingly never-ending cycle of abandonment flows from one generation to the next. The absence of the Black man in the household and community is a heart wrenching reality felt very often by Black women. More times than not, the Black woman has no choice except to be the mother and the father to her children. Not having the Black man in the household leaves a never-ending hole of abandonment that forms from the emptiness, low self-esteem, insecurities, and worthlessness the woman and her children might feel. The often-asked question is: Why do so many Black men abandon their women and their children? The historical timeline shows that the vast majority of Black men are either behind prison bars or dead. Unlike many other races, the Black race wasn't fortunate enough to escape injustice and racism. The Black family has been split apart since slavery over 400 years ago and still is to this day, due to various reasons. Fatherless daughters and fatherless sons are left to deal with life alone. According to Statistica, "In 2018, there were about 4.04 million Black families in the United States with a single mother. This is an increase from 1990 levels, when there were about 3.4 million Black families with a single mother." (Duffin, 2019) Abandonment is often decided before brown babies depart from their mother's womb.

You Can Survive; I Did

by Thelma Marigna-Shaw

They say words have power when you speak into your life; good and strong words are positive. I call that self-talk. I've learned to be my own cheerleader. I've been thinking about all I've been dealing with throughout my life. I figured out that I was dealing with the issues of *"abandonment"* that took place all throughout my life.

The very first time I recall *"abandonment"* in my life was when my mom and dad would leave me at a very young age and go shopping or to church, which was next door to our house. I remember one of my first beatings was because I went downstairs and made myself something to eat and burned my arm. That is only because a "sister got hungry." Now you know that's a shame that I was able to fix my own food at that age.

I was always a daddy's girl through and through. I traveled and went everywhere I could with my dad. Then one year we went to Chicago to visit my dad's sister. Little did I know I was getting dropped off. Yep! My dad left me with Aunt Verdell. That broke my heart. *"Abandonment"* struck my life all over again. Aunt Verdell took good care of me. She never had children of her own, so she spoiled me rotten. Even though she spoiled me, I still had emptiness in my heart for my dad.

On February 18, 1971, *"abandonment"* hit me with the death of my beloved father. I feel that this was the first time I was ever truly *"abandoned."* This is the hurt that your soul cries from. The reality that I would never physically see him again was so overwhelming that I tried to get into the casket the day of his funeral. I've always dreamed how my life would have been if my father had been here to send me off to prom, or see me graduate, and most of all having him walk me down the aisle on my wedding day. My father was my protector and if he was living, he would have never given his blessing for me to marry my first husband.

This brings me to the *"abandonment"* that I faced in my marriage; after 20 years, my husband walked out. I was a young married woman to a man who provided for me and our children. The first 10 years of our marriage was ok. After 10 years of marriage, my husband's role model, his father, passed away. From that point, our marriage went on a downward spiral, leading to our divorce. This was both rejection as well as *"abandonment"* at its worst. I couldn't believe it. I felt like not only did he leave, but where was God! I've always been a woman of God. As the storm became almost unbearable, it was my faith in God and my children that kept me grounded.

I found that the mortgage had not been paid for months, and I was faced with eviction notices. I was unemployed and displaced with nowhere for me and my children to live; that was our new reality. I felt worthless. I felt like I was the biggest

17

mess up in the world. I was always in church praying and serving the Lord and working in the community. Now, everyone was looking at me. I was so totally embarrassed. I would overhear people saying, "Did you hear about sister Major." How did this happen to me? I had hit rock bottom, I had to call on the Lord like I never had before. I cried, prayed, and fasted asking God to direct my path. I needed Him to open some doors for me and my children.

To feel yourself on the potter's wheel was far from easy, but through God's grace and mercy, I was able to endure the process. Things began to turn around for the better. I was blessed with two new jobs and a new home for me and my children. The greatest gift of all was the new church family that embraced me and my children. Needless to say, it is amazing to reflect back on the storm God brought me through.

I was a daughter first, and then a wife but my greatest achievement in life was being a mother. When I held my youngest son for the first time and looked at his little face, I wanted the world for him. He had a smile that would change the whole room, and when I looked into his eyes it was with such brightness and happiness. His eyes were filled with life. He turned into an amazing young man, filled with hope and a bright future. Then one day, he took the pen I gave him and began to write his own story. I still remember the day I looked into his eyes as the sheriff's deputies handcuffed him and took him away from me. At that moment a part of me died. My heart was so broken, I collapsed into a chair; my heart was torn into so many pieces. My son didn't abandon me, but it sure felt like it. It was the choices he made that hurt me so bad. It gets scary sometimes and with him not being present hurts to an unbearable point more than words can describe. There were times when I felt *"abandoned"*. There were days when I didn't want to get out of bed.

Fast forward to now. I had to face losing my best friend. My mother was my living shero. Her story for me was inspiring to me. She was raised a farm girl, and she dealt with the agony and pain of being raped at the young age of 13. She was made to give up her child. My mother made up her mind to never be a victim again, which led her to become a pistol packing toting woman! She worked very hard to pull herself up out of the red clay hills of Alabama to the tops of the Colorado Rocky Mountains, where I would watch her go from scrubbing White folks' floors, to doing private duty nursing in their homes. She was a strong God-fearing woman. That is where I got my strong faith values. There were so many times when I wanted to be just like her. After she passed away, I realized that God created me in His image to be used by Him. He has His own plan for me. Even though I have faced multiple *"abandonment"* issues throughout my life, I have turned into a living testimony on how you can overcome any obstacles with strong faith. Not saying you will never face issues, but God will bring you through. My God is bigger than *"abandonment."*

END

WATCH FOR

- **The willingness to put up with anything just to avoid being alone**
- **You have internalized the trauma and it caused insecurity issues**
- **Look for reasons to leave**
- **Moving on too quickly or jumping into new relationships to quickly**

POVERTY

Mother and daughter in the neighborhood

How is it that America is one of the richest countries in the world, yet nearly half of single Black mothers and their children live in poverty? *"They got money for wars, but can't feed the poor." (Tupac Shakur, 1993)* Poverty comes in different forms: Situational, generational, absolute, relative, rural and, most commonly known, urban.

An example is the struggling Black woman who works three or four jobs and is a single mother doing the best she can while raising her children alone. Then, there are the infamous welfare Black women who stand in line at the welfare building and only know the system. Tupac Shakur said it best: *"I give a holler to my sisters on welfare, Tupac cares, if don't nobody else cares and uh, I know they like to beat ya down a lot when you come around the block brothas clown a lot, but please don't cry, dry your eyes, never let up, forgive but don't forget, girl keep your head up." (Tupac Shakur, 1993)*

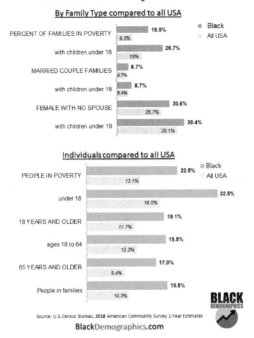

Black Poverty Rates

By Family Type compared to all USA

- PERCENT OF FAMILIES IN POVERTY — Black 18.5%, All USA 9.3%
- with children under 18 — Black 26.7%, All USA 15%
- MARRIED COUPLE FAMILIES — Black 6.7%, All USA 4.7%
- with children under 18 — Black 8.7%, All USA 6.4%
- FEMALE WITH NO SPOUSE — Black 30.6%, All USA 25.7%
- with children under 18 — Black 39.4%, All USA 35.1%

Individuals compared to all USA

- PEOPLE IN POVERTY — Black 22.5%, All USA 13.1%
- under 18 — Black 32.5%, All USA 18.0%
- 18 YEARS AND OLDER — Black 19.1%, All USA 11.7%
- ages 18 to 64 — Black 19.5%, All USA 12.3%
- 65 YEARS AND OLDER — Black 17.0%, All USA 9.4%
- People in families — Black 19.8%, All USA 10.3%

Source: U.S. Census Bureau, 2018 American Community Survey 1-Year Estimates

BlackDemographics.com

As the chart above shows, when considering Black families with and without children who live below the national poverty line, the vast majority (74% or 1.4 million) are headed by single women, and just 16% are headed by a married-couple family. Only 10% are headed by a single father.

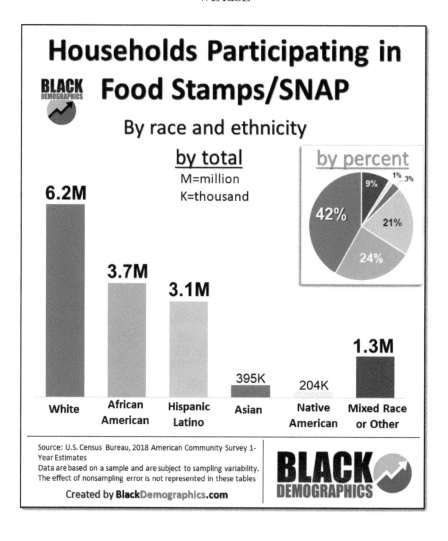

Households Participating in Food Stamps/SNAP

By race and ethnicity

Despite running stereotypes that associate African Americans with being the primary consumers of the SNAP program, formerly known as and commonly referred to as the Food Stamp program, White Americans are actually the primary benefactors of this program. In 2018, there were 3.7 million African American households participating in SNAP/Food Stamps (24%) compared to 6.2 million White households who make up 42% of total households using SNAP/Food Stamps. However, when adjusted for population Black households do use

SNAP/Food Stamps at a higher rate. This also means that contrary to similar stereotypical narratives the majority of Black households do not use SNAP/Food Stamps.

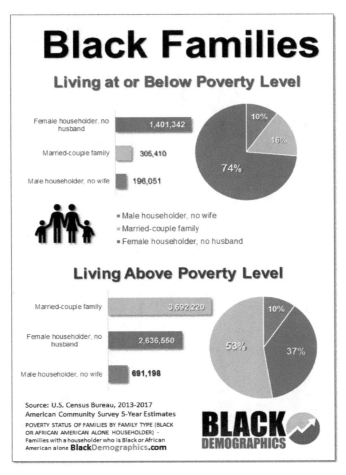

Still Undefeated

by Sharolin Sanders

I was a young Black girl living a regular life in Pennsylvania with my mother, four brothers and one sister. Just that fast, I was 6 years old, living with my grandmother and two older brothers in my hometown of Orange, N.J. My mother said she was going to come back. She did. My very last moments with her happened when I was seven. She shook me out of my sleep in the middle of the night and took my older brothers and me to White Castle. Later, I found out she had got into some trouble and was deported to her home country of Jamaica. Grandma was a traditional

Jamaican woman. Discipline was key; she was strict, no TV during school days, chores, Christian radio and just books no toys.

I was 12 when I was awakened with lashes from a shade opener. It wasn't my first whoopin' but it was the worst. I felt like it was my fault because I came home late with my oldest brother after basketball practice. I didn't feel safe walking home alone, so I went to where he was and waited until he was ready. It was well after 12 when we got home, so I knew she was really worried about me. The next day we had church; we had a ride waiting for us. It was on a snowy morning when my older brother was out early to make some money by shoveling driveways that a lady paid him in AA batteries, and he was mad about it. It was cold and Grandma told him to get a jacket on, but he refused. She swung and nailed him right in the nose. He started bleeding and ran out of the car. He ushered that Sunday with bruised arms; it was so hard to move.

Around 8 pm, we got a knock on the door. It was my brother, the Police, and a lady. She asked me questions for hours. I didn't want to get my grandma in trouble, so I lied, but the honest answers were on my arms and legs.

After all the questions we packed a few outfits and went to the hospital for a couple of hours, and then we were sent into a home. I was still thinking about my grandma, and my 6th grade basketball season but my thoughts were not the same thoughts the Department of Youth and Family Services (DYFS) was thinking, I wanted to go home. After that night, we were removed from that home together, and I was placed separately. From then on, I was alone from what I was used to being around daily: No grandma, no brothers, no basketball; just me. I shut down, stayed silent, stayed to myself, was hungry, and didn't socialize in school. They removed me from that home after three months, and from then on that seemed to be the sequence until I was in high school, and I moved in with an interracial family.

I was bounced around to 12 foster homes and one group home. I had to get used to 12 different families, nine different schools, including being homeschooled while living in Brahma House, and about six different caseworkers. Amongst six workers, three of my favorites were Black women. During those times, I felt alone and unloved, because I liked some of the homes, but my caseworkers never gave me a good reason as to why I had to leave. In a few cases, I wanted to leave, but my caseworkers didn't hear my cry until I got rebellious, a side they rarely saw. Through those situations, I was having a hard time finding myself, a family, and what love really meant.

Mainly living with White families, I thought I would never see Black again until I lived with one interracial family. The mom was Black, and the dad was White. I had never seen that before but for the first time I saw Black being normalized without feeling different. My foster mother would go to bat for my Blackness. I started having issues with White teachers at school.

They would tell me I had to take off my headband. She called the school and told them "no that's her hairstyle." Although living there didn't work out until this day she always included me in her Black family. I was 17 and on my way to College of Saint Elizabeth when an old caseworker introduced this opportunity with a non-profit organization where I can travel to Africa to showcase my talent, coach, teach basketball, and live and learn in the African culture. For two years I traveled to 6 different countries in Africa for basketball with beautiful Black women.

Being that I was living mostly with White folks since I was 12, it was a culture shock to see that many Black women. Throughout college, I was learning how to be Black again, how to do my hair, and about Black culture, Black history, the Black panthers, everything Black! I was in an identity crisis. It's not something anyone prepared me for. I didn't know I was attracted to women. Being a gay Black woman was not normal to me until I saw other gay Black women. Meanwhile, one of my caseworkers was a gay Black woman. It was something I didn't speak about because I just didn't know what that feeling was. I never had a real connection to a man, not even as a father figure but liking women is what felt natural to me. I was in college, and I felt free to be me. I can like what I like and not be looked at as if I had something on my face, and these other gay women were here for me to relate to.

I realized that being gay was hard for other people to adjust to. One night, after not seeing a girl, I was dating all summer, I brought her home. I was living with my grandma again. I was just about to lay down and go to sleep. My grandma came into the room and simply said "she's not staying here." So, we broke all rules and went back to CSE for the night. My thoughts were that my brother has White girls here all the time, so what could be the issue. Not feeling the love from my grandma, I would come back for clothes, food and toiletries. I basically made my car my home in my new church's parking lot. Still having to make money by Ubering, I was depressed thinking nothing in my life is going well and asking why it was hard for my own people just to accept me for me. For six months, night after night, I slept in the car unharmed and unbothered. Thank God. Church folks would park their cars and wave, some would see what I'm up to, but it was never a question of "Why are you here all the time?" Nobody knew I was struggling, because I always kept clean and never looked like what I was going through; it was really hell. After I overcame all those obstacles, I realized I wasn't meant to be defeated. My God made me strong enough to face every battle and handle challenges according to his word. He has ordered my steps since day one, and I thank Him every day for making me the strong Black woman that I have grown to be.

END

Curious children in a Washington, D.C. neighborhood

Although some Black women abuse the government assistance they receive, many Black women rarely make what little assistance they receive stretch the full course of the month. The government focuses solely on putting Black women on welfare or getting them jobs instead of encouraging their pursuit toward gaining more education. Geographically, every major city in America has an outlined low-income section. These low-income communities were often designed to separate along race and socioeconomic class. These communities were best known as the "slums". The term "slum" is often used to depict overcrowded, unhealthy and limited to basic services like running water, window accessibility, plumbing and sewage, and electricity. Some might refer to these impoverished communities as "hoods" or "the ghettos". These communities often lack educational, recreational and many health resources and are many times entrenched with violence, drugs and crime. This geographic segregation outline has continued long after "The Great Migration". As we take a look at historical framework practices to keep Blacks in lower income communities, we will get to truly see how not much has changed since slavery.

Let's start in the beginning. During slavery, the slaves lived in "slave quarters". After slavery ended, around 1916 many slaves migrated north, this was titled as "The Great Migration". During this migration of Black families many moved into apartment buildings, and the ones who stayed in the south moved to all Black segregated communities called the "slums". In 1935, President Roosevelt signed the Social Security Act. People fell into one of three programs under the Social Security Act, which includes Social Security, the unemployment insurance system, or the dependent childhood program (ADC), currently known as Aid to Families with Dependent Children (ADFC). The government-built communities for poor people and housed them all together. One of the government housing systems is called "the projects," which are usually highly overly populated with low-income families. These same low-income communities lack educational as well as recreational resources. The housing projects, for example, were never designed to get Black people on their feet to become future homeowners. The system created by the government was orchestrated to keep Blacks in a never-ending cycle of poverty and crime. America did not want Black people to become self-sufficient homeowners but instead we were exposed to welfare and acclimated to be dependent on the tax dollars of the middle class. Throughout real estate history "racial steering" and "redlining" kept Black people from ever becoming homeowners. The term "racial steering" refers to the practice that real estate brokers would use when advising customers to purchase homes in certain areas based on race. Another practice to continue community racial segregation was "redlining". The discriminatory term "redlining" is the practice of keeping certain ethnic groups from receiving fair treatment when looking to buy a home. In some instances, this practice can be seen in denial of mortgages, loans, insurance solely based on location rather than the applicants' qualifications. More and more property and land were acquired by people not of color throughout the 1900s and still often today until *"But one percent of the people in this country control seventy percent of the wealth." (Assata Shakur, 1987)*

WEB Dubois once vocalized, "If they had been given an economic start at Emancipation, if they had been in an enlightened and rich community which really desired their best good, then we might perhaps call such a result small or even insignificant." (WEB DuBois, 1903) According to sources African Americans had the highest poverty rate, 27.4 percent. *Did we as Black people ask for poverty?* Did we ask to live in project buildings one on top of the other? WEB DuBois said it best, *"It's not an image we have, it's an image we were given." (WEB DuBois, 1903)*

So many Black families have been living in poverty for so many generations they don't even know how to change. *"Compressed ghettos threaten to explode. Poverty and fire and brimstone boil over into deadly stew, but the "beautiful" people refuse to let me read in peace." (Assata Shakur, 1987)* Despair is the only way of living known to countless Black families. So, the temporary fix to this long-term lack of economic stability is crime which leads to violence, resulting in incarceration and or death. The cycle of despair just repeats itself in the Black community, *"Black people are oppressed because of class as well as race, because we are poor and because we are Black." Assata Shakur, 1987)*

How do we as Black women break the chains of poverty that still have so many of us bound? The key to closing the poverty gap is simply education. Despite being surrounded with struggle, Black women can overcome any obstacle set before her. A Black woman's skillful resourcefulness is extremely extraordinary and is one of the major characteristics that make her so unique. Black American's buy land and pass it down one generation to the next. Stop spending money on trends and start investing in property.

WAYS TO EMPOWER YOURSELF OUT OF POVERTY

- Education
- Transportation
- Employment
- Build Credit
- Save Money

My Spirit Free

by Angelique Terry-Tricoche

Who has four kids with the intention of raising them alone? Who has four kids before they are old enough to get carded at a nightclub? Better yet, who has four kids by a guy who gets them pregnant, stays gone a year only to return and get her pregnant again and again?

Yes, that was me. I was the silly young girl in this nightmare scenario, who chose to procreate before creating a life of my own or even knowing what that meant. As messed up as it sounds, I am sure that I am not alone in this experience, there are countless other young women, past and present, who may live in this reality. They are women like me who at some point during our difficult childhood got this notion in our minds that since we were not born into an ideal family unit, we would create one for ourselves, minus the dysfunction. Unfortunately, we soon find out that this thought process alone is dysfunctional and far removed from reality, yet we fight hard to make this lie that comes from a place of ignorance, innocence and desperation become true. However, the truth always wins in these situations, and we end up facing the reality that life is not a fairytale, nor is it a dream.

For me, this was the beginning of a struggle that I had only dreamed of a few years prior. These dreams were far different than the ones I had when I was little. Before that, I lived in a world full of imaginations and dreams of my own making; I was always looking for a way to escape my reality. Both of my parents had dealt with their own personal struggles and as a result, I was left to fend for myself in a lot of ways. Honestly, I do not blame them for thinking I could handle things because I was the kind of kid who seemed naturally inclined to wisdom, an insightful child prone to having good judgment.

I can recall at the tender age of five, after spending a few days with my grandmother, who had not heard from my mom, so she decided to get in her car with me and to try to find out where she was. She only knew the general direction of the apartment my mom and I had just moved into, but she did not have the correct address. I told her I knew how to get there, and she had confidence that I could. I was too little to see out of the window, so she let me climb onto the center console where I was able to lead the way. Once we parked and walked into the building then up the elevator to the correct apartment number, she knocked, and my mom opened the door looking like she had been crying. She told my grandmother that she and her boyfriend had been deported for fighting and that she was tired of working two jobs and just struggling in general. My grandmother told me to go to my room and get my dress shoes because we would be going to church the next morning. So, I did as I was told, but right before we left, I gave my mom a hug and told her, she did not need that man or that job, all she needed was Jesus!

So that was me in a nutshell, always the responsible kid, cleaning up without being told, cooking for myself and sometimes my mom, always trying to make good grades and please everyone around me. I had my struggles like any kid, but I never wanted to be a problem for anyone. That was until I was 12. I remember becoming angry and disillusioned by all my efforts to please everyone else. No one was changing for me! My mom and dad were so busy trying to figure themselves out that my wellbeing was an afterthought. I remember prior to that dreaming of becoming a model one day and a singer the next. I would practice my singing in front of anyone who would listen. Some days, I wanted to be a writer and an artist and spent a lot of time writing stories, songs and drawing pictures. By the time I was fourteen, it seemed to me that my childhood dreams had died. I had become cynical and disillusioned; I was discouraged at seeing so many of my prayers go unanswered and nothing but chaos around me that I just gave up hope. If I was not going to have the kind of family stability, I felt I deserved, I was going to create it for myself. That is when I started to have new dreams, dreams about boys, about a boy, about an imaginary future husband and children.

"I want twins, a boy and a girl; that's all [the kids] I want," I would say to anyone who would listen. I even prayed to God in earnest that He would bless me with this request.

So, without any real contemplation and only a dream about what I wanted to do I set out to use the one thing that I knew would get the ball rolling, my body. I found that "boy" who could make all my dreams come true. He was cute, I liked him, he pursued me, so we started having, poorly protected, ill-informed, adolescent sex. I got pregnant the very first time. Then as previously stated, between one tumultuous situation after another, I got pregnant two more times. First, we had a boy, then a girl and as if that weren't enough for the both of us who were from dysfunctional families, we were blessed with those twins I had prayed for a few years earlier, a boy and a girl. And that was the only thing we both had accomplished at that point in our lives, me the girl and him the boy who without any type of plan, creating babies and that was a family in my young mind. Prior to having those babies, I didn't lend any real thought to a plan of action, like where would we live? How would we make money? What about childcare? I had no concept of any of the things that an adult would consider before making major life decisions. And how could I make any of those responsible choices, when after all I was still a child, a damaged child trying to create a better life without a clue about how to make that happen.

At some point, I began to realize this was far from the fairytale I thought it would be. We fought, broke up, got back together, had sex, drank, smoked, and did whatever destructive behaviors I had witnessed throughout my young life at the time. My poor babies looked well on the outside because if there was one thing my mother taught me was how to keep up appearances. But we were "buck-wild." He was so inclined to destruction that he decided to take his poor decisions across state lines under the guise of "making money" he stayed gone a lot. I lived between my mother's house, relatives, and grandparents and sometimes in my own apartment. There was no way I could get a good job without my high school diploma, so I worked part-time for minimum wage and relied on welfare while attempting to go back to school. At some point during that time, we grew apart; not really, it was because he got himself locked up and so I moved clear across the country from Los Angeles to the east coast with my mom and her new husband and his children, from a previous relationship.

We lived together in the normal chaotic lifestyle I became accustomed to. I took a job in a hospital records department at night to provide for my kids and things seemed to be going okay. My stepdad drove trucks and often went out of state most times my mom went with him. So, that left my new siblings in charge of watching my children while I was at work.

Now before I go any further into this part of my story, let me make this one plea to the mothers of young children; DO NOT trust anyone around your kids! Or at least be extremely cautious about those you choose to care for your children. If need be, leave them with a close relative or someone you are certain you can trust to protect them, someone not oblivious to the dangers that exist in this cruel and wicked world. Never leave them with older teens or friends that have children older than yours especially when you don't know their background. One would think I would have learned this from my own childhood, but unfortunately, I had to be reminded through an experience of two of my own. Some life lessons are hard, but the hardest lessons come from the realization that your poor choices as a parent, could negatively affect those little people you wouldn't hesitate to give your life for, your children. Upon learning that my child had been harmed I was devastated, once again my normally crazy world had been turned upside down. Dreams were long gone and now I was truly living a nightmare that I had not bargained for.

I sank so low, I felt like I would never get up off the ground again. I had been through bad situations before but now that I was trying to do better and to be a better mother, daughter, and sister to my new siblings, I found myself on the floor, knocked down by life again. It was in this low moment that I began to realize something had been missing from my life for some time. Something that I knew I always had which was my faith. It was a foundation that I had ever since I was that innocent five-year-old girl telling my mom who it was that she needed more than anything or anyone, it was Jesus. He had seen me through so many struggles that I know I would not have made it through on my own. I realized that I could no longer rely on my grandmother's prayers alone but that I needed to have a new relationship with Him for myself. And that is when I really began to do the hard work.

I had new resolve; I was no longer going to use the excuse that I was too young to really live this "churchy" kind of lifestyle. I wanted a future for my children that was better than the one I had. Most importantly, I realized that I needed to break every generational spirit that had attached itself to me before I was born, especially the ones now trying to destroy my children. I started praying more and searching the word of God every day. I went to church and took my babies with me. I started growing stronger and being more attentive to my children. I focused on their education, their healing and well-being more and for that the Lord really began to bless my life. My outlook started to change, and I began to dream again, only this time I allowed the Lord to give me the dreams He had for me. He showed me the kind of opportunities my children would have in being made whole and that they would enjoy being kids. I saw them begin to thrive knowing that they were protected and that no matter what their mom would always be there to care for them, to hear them, to be present with them.

Only the Holy Spirit could do these things for me, to me and through me. I am not going to say that things were always smooth sailing, we struggled, but I had a different assurance deep down on the inside. I was being made new, I had joy, and I was free. I was no longer the girl who gave up on her dreams, they just came with new perspectives, and they are alive inside of me once again.

I kept my kids involved with sports and focused on their academics. I did school projects and attended teacher parent conferences. They did well in school and grew to become some of the most respectful and pleasant human beings. They have their struggles, but nothing is too hard for God. By His grace, my kids became the first in my immediate family to attend and graduate from high school on time and then to go off to college. I too went back and finished school, getting my GED. I have almost completed my degree, I am now a wife to an amazing minister of the gospel who loves my children as his own, we added one more precious jewel to our family, and she is wonderful. I am an entrepreneur and homeowner. Through Jesus Christ, I became an overcomer! He took my broken pieces and made me, my children, my mother, and even my father before he passed, whole. He shined his light in and on our lives and we are free; we are free indeed.

END

SACRIFICE

"And I realize momma really paid the price, she nearly gave her life, to raise me right" (Tupac Shakur, 1993)

The true meaning of sacrifice plays a great deal in a Black woman's life and is exemplified all throughout history, where they have sacrificed their time, health, and lives. It is part of a Black woman's natural instincts to sacrifice for the better. Families being separated on the auction block during slavery turned on the inner switch for a Black woman to become the head of the family. In America, Black women head many households. As a result, these same women no longer have the time to better themselves. Data has shown that 85% of Asian children live with two married parents, as is the case for the majority of White children; 74% of them live in a two-parent household. In 2015, studies show that less than 36% of Black children live in a two-parent married household. The blueprint of family structure was torn apart for Black people as a whole during slavery. Black mothers and fathers ripped away from their children and each other created the division within Black families that still affects us to the present day. The lack of education in the Black community resorts in lack of information about sexual and reproductive health and rights. The family and community so customarily lack presence in a child's life so that resorts to a wide range of outcomes.

There is a pattern of unplanned pregnancy in low-income communities. Teen pregnancy falls under the unplanned pregnancy categorization. The vast majority of teen pregnancy among Black teens is between the ages of fifteen and eighteen years of age. Some call this, babies having babies. Society has a way of blaming teen pregnancy on the race, although the race is not to blame, but instead the society that was built to keep Black people in lower income, impoverished communities, constructed for them to fail.

Research has shown that single Black mothers in America make up 65% of the single mother population. Single Black mothers lead the fight against surviving the culture of poverty. The repeated absence of a father and the presence of single mothers have become the predictable outcome in the Black culture. Unplanned teen pregnancy is one of the more common sacrifices made by young Black women. Tupac Shakur said in his poem, Tears of a Teenage Mother "He's bragging about his new Jordans the Baby just ran out of milk he's buying gold every 2 weeks the Baby just ran out of Pampers He's buying clothes for his new girl & the Daddy just ran out the Door."

When the Black woman attempts to juggle getting an education and being a mother, oftentimes being a mother wins. The drop out cycle is due to the ongoing learned dysfunction attached to children of teen mothers who are more likely to have lower school achievement and drop out of high school. (CDC, 2017)

Many times, young Black women find themselves trapped and decide to make decisions such as dropping out of school after having a baby. The drop-out rate for African Americans is three times higher than the amount of two or more races and Whites. Many young Black girls who find themselves pregnant as a teenager have to make the ultimate educational sacrifice, they drop out of school. This has been many young teen mothers greatest sacrifice in their earliest years after becoming a new mother. In 2016, approximately 2.3 million youth between the ages of 16-24 years old were not enrolled in high school and had not yet received a high school diploma or Graduate Equivalency Degree (GED).

The Black student population makes up 6.3% of that 2.3 million. One of the leading causes is due to underfunding, which causes the students to be least likely to receive the best learning. This is a major issue in the Black community, the lack of funding for education has been one of the leading reasons youth turn to crime and a life of violence. As Black mothers in these instances have to sit back and see their children now, they have to repeat the cycle, all because that is a very difficult thing to unlearn.

Single Black mothers battle repeatedly with surviving poverty, lack of resources, and lack of employment in their communities. They manage to balance the world on their shoulders. The majority of Black women habitually have been conditioned to put themselves last just so they can take care of everything and everyone else.

The Strength to Bounce Back

by Annika Brown

From a very young age, I have had downfalls after downfalls. These events in my life pushed me into a position where I had to learn how to regain my strength and bounce back.

The first downfall I can remember that had my face in the mud was getting pregnant at 14. This event affected my entire family and the reputation we had in our community.

This was the typical peer pressure situation that I fell into. Everyone had a boyfriend; I wanted one too, never taking into consideration everything that comes with having one, i.e., the possibility of a baby. The news spread far and wide about my pregnancy. This put so much weight on my self-esteem and my emotions. I felt like a total failure: I had committed the ultimate crime and there is no redemption for me. Somehow, I found the strength to keep going, pulling myself out the bed each day, performing my new tasks as a mother. It took strength that I had no idea I had. After a year of mustering up the strength to live, to bounce back, here comes baby number two. Talk about the ultimate failure. The word on the street was "Her life is over, she has no future, she will never go anywhere or do anything."

The reality of my situation hit even harder when I met people on the street that knew, and they would look the other way, or walked by students my age with my babies strapped to me, and they would all laugh. If you have never wished the earth would open up and take you in, I have. All my dreams at this point just seemed to be something in a book that would never happen. My strength was fading again, and the days were as gloomy as could be. I thought to myself, "Can I ever find the strength to bounce back from this double dilemma?" My aunt said to me the day after praying for me, "Once there is life, there is hope."

That became the driving force or the fuel I needed to get up and try again. Try life again; bounce back from this downfall and any to come. If I can still breath, there is a decision I can make to get back up and try again. I was behind on all things academic, so I needed the strength to work twice as hard to catch up to those in my age group. That strength carried through the process of reaching 23 years old. That was one of my proudest moments. They said I couldn't and wouldn't be able to. I wanted to make sure that my children would have a way better future than I had, and just having a GED was not going to do that for them. I thought to myself again, can I defy what they said about me and actually get a career? This was going to take so much strength to pull this one off. I'm still behind, I thought to myself. Yeah, but once there is life there is hope, I told myself, and if you found the strength to accomplish and check off GED on your list, for sure you can do this. This bounce is going to take quite a bit of force.

A year went by and yes, I was able to check off my career when I became a licensed practical nurse. It is amazing how checking off your goals list can give momentum to keep going. They told me I could not do it, but here I am. Got my GED and graduated from nursing school. I found the strength and I bounced back. Can I push it any further I thought? Can this teen mom have a double career under her belt despite the odds? Once there is life there is hope. I went back to school, chasing an associate degree in human resources. This one was tough, working full time, family full time, and going to school. This one took strength I really did not know I had. Finally, it was over, and I had something new to hang on the wall. Yes, today I hold an associate degree in human resources. After everything they said about me, I found the strength to bounce back.

WE RISE

2

Faithfulness & Relationships

Church mothers

"Faith means being sure of the things we hope for. And faith means knowing that something is real even if we do not see it" (Heb. 11:1)

The heart and soul of a Black woman is infused with the faith she has always stood on. Black women have always been recognized for their strength in God. Don't get me wrong; we are not angels. The Black woman's faith has uplifted entire villages and been the glue to keep families and communities together, *"The Church often stands as a real conserver of morals, a strengthener of family life, and the final authority on what is God and Right." (WEB Du Bois, 1903)*

Aspiration to Alignment

by The Rev. Staci Williams

That's it; count em...it took me twelve Long-Long-Long years to earn my bachelor's degree!!! I would love to say that the journey was filled with milestones and epiphanies, but that simply would not be the truth. While there were many lessons learned and experiences gained, the fact of the matter is that a lot of my scenic routes were fueled off rebellion, pride and my unwillingness to listen to sound advice. Let's go back to 1997.

In 1997, I was working for a popular hotel chain. Three years in, I was certain to be promoted to a supervisory position. Well, that time never came. In fact, I was constantly overlooked by others and left to train the ones that were being placed over me. After being "Dissed" for the THIRD TIME, I decided to go to management and ask some questions. Without stuttering my manager, with her West Indian accent, looked at me and said, "You have no college degree!" Man, that stung, because I was actually in school struggling through my sixth year and third attempt. I said, "Don't I get credit for trying?" She replied, "You get encouragement for trying and rewarded once you finish." Well, that dialogue certainly pivoted my thinking. Up until that point I believed if I worked hard enough and strived for excellence within the workplace, I would get acknowledged appropriately! Boy, was I wrong...or was I actually, right???

Eventually, I had to get out of my feelings and make some decisions. I had to complete school. My true hurdle was overcoming a severe tendency to procrastinate and paying my tuition. Obviously, these two ideals left unmanaged are recipes for disasters. But I was a thinker. I decided to make a BOSS move and in September 1998, I QUIT!!!! I figured I would place all my efforts into looking for a job that had tuition reimbursement and pick up a couple of courses at the local Community College. Well, I'm three weeks in on my new journey and everything has stalemated. I had no job prospects; I could not afford the classes and I was borderline DEPRESSED!

Please understand that admitting to showing signs of Depression was taboo. I mean, with all this "LIFE" going on, I was also this young preacher. I was placed on platforms to be an example and a chief encouragement to my peers. And, while I smiled for the cameras and knew my queue, I felt like a FRAUD! How could I ever admit that my Faith was beginning to fail?

Sitting in my room one day, there was a knock. My mother entered in with that "I'm about to change your LIFE" look. She looked at me, while trying to control the disappointment in her eyes, and said, "Staci, you have made good and bad choices." She continued saying, "Your biggest issue is your refusal to LISTEN...Hear me and hear me good...Some women "GET IT" at 25 and some "GET IT" at 40...I pray you don't wait until you are 40!" While harsh and a bit confusing, for some reason these words felt like a seed falling into a prepared ground.

On November 9, 1998, those words aka seed yielded its fruit. I got a new JOB!!! With this job, I had an official title, Health Benefits, 401K and Tuition

Reimbursement. I began to learn many different facets of the Mortgage Industry and was quickly becoming one of the highest producers. Within the next year I was promoted twice. And, while everything seemed to be going well, my school endeavors were placed on the back burner. I was actually resolved at that point; my initial school of thought of working hard and getting rewarded in the workplace was actually paying off. I began to have ASPIRATIONS beyond my immediate leadership team and started seeing myself as one of the BIG BOSSES!! I started taking in-house classes, creating reports and job aides. I had to prove that I had what it took to LEAD!! But it started happening again – other "Team Players" were promoted over me because I had no DEGREE!!

That was the last straw – I returned to LaSalle University, buckled down and in 2003, I earned my BA in Criminal Justice and Sociology. Excited about this milestone – I began applying for different positions and shortly thereafter became a SUPERVISOR!!!

I'm good, feeling great, living my best life and decided to post for another Supervisor position that came with a 10K pay increase. Guess what? I got that position too!!! Oh, I'm unstoppable. I have the degree, experience, proven record of success and the respect of my peers. What could go wrong? Well, one day I came home from work and was called into a family meeting. My mom notified me that she had been diagnosed with Breast Cancer. Needless to say, this news put me into a temporary state of shock, to say the least. I remember as I began to come to, I felt the urgency to just start praying. I mean that is what we do, RIGHT??? Keep in mind that through the Graduation and Promotions, I was also a PREACHER! I knew God had called me to a KINGDOM ASSIGNMENT; I just felt that it was for later.

Through her recovery process my prayers developed, and I felt that I was drawing even closer to God. Up until this point, the trials that I faced were usually self-induced. Now, I'm witnessing the struggle of my mother's diagnosis. I needed

God's voice to be louder than the screaming I heard in my head. As time went on, I could feel the depth of God's love towards me. I was a little worried. While I was praying that God would heal my mother, the extra time in His presence revealed some things within me.

One of the things that were revealed was the importance of being willing to STRETCH into new and hard places. I took this revelation and made it work within the workplace. Part of my duty in taking care of my mom was assisting with her CSF shots. In order to do this, I had to work remotely on certain days. Trying to be the diligent Leader, I tried my best to maintain a presence within the operations of my team – even when I wasn't there physically. One day, I was called into my manager's office and was told that the level of involvement I had with my team remotely, bought into question if my mother really was that SICK. Now, I don't quite remember what my exact words were in response, but I will say, our work relationship NEVER RECOVERED!! In fact, she enacted a plan to strip me from my team and put me on the chopping block for the next layoff.

Within six months I found myself being handed a proposed Release Letter and Severance Package. In essence, I was told that a Newer, Less Experienced, No Degree having, White – Blond Hair Supervisor was hired to take my place. My previous experience with perceived racism had a camouflaged undertone. This incident was BOLD and was almost daring me to call it out. While completely pissed, I found myself going back to GOD. I remember crying and asking if there will EVER be anything in my life that will be seamless and drama free. Why do I constantly have to deal with this Corporate Bull Crap!!! All I wanted to do is WORK HARD and GET PAID for doing it!!

With a few written letters, meetings and interviews, my company saw the label on the wall. About two weeks before my Termination Date, I was assigned to be the Supervisor of another Department. I was placed with a team that was infamous for failing and had no promising upswing. Initially, I thought I was being set-up to justify their previous attempt to terminate me. Well, the challenge of this position turned in my FAVOR. Because of the success of the team, I was given different accolades and eventually was promoted to Manager. Oh, did I mention that my previous manager was placed on probation and eventually released. Yes, the enemy actually became my FOOTSTOOL!!!

Before we move forward let me provide some quick fill-in details: I have 11 years at my company; I earned an MBA in Finance, was promoted to Operations Manager and was installed as the Pastor of Garden of Prayer Church – NJ. In this season – I remember being very reflective and humbled about God's continued favor extended towards me. I was on the path to NEXT LEVEL happiness – but why did I still feel so empty? Why was I still experiencing feelings of unfulfillment?

Fast-forward to 2013, I'm a year in as Ops Manager and I have just added accounting as a supplemental concentration to my MBA. Surely, this was going to lead to an Executive Position. Well, in May 2013, my mom's health began to decline, and on Friday, August 2nd at 2:38 a.m., she became My Angel. While holding my mother's hands during her closing hours, I began to make promises regarding the church. Oh, I forgot to mention that while my mother was never the Pastor of Garden of Prayer Church in New Jersey, she is recorded as its Founder. The day she gained her wings, a MANTEL was transferred. I knew that the promises that I was making were going to require a deeper level of sacrifice. Less than two months after my mom's transition, I made the decision to walk away from my 15-Year Career and enter into Full-Time Ministry. It's funny because discussing this decision with my Director, he knew that based on what he witnessed at my Mother's home-going, I would not be with the company much longer.

Taking this step, I was filled with all kinds of emotions. My Faith began to evolve in ways that surpassed fancy clichés and gimmicks. God literally began to reveal to me what it was to have LIVING FAITH. For clarity, let's define the verb form of FAITH as having absolute trust and belief in God's ability. Using this definition, I had to leap into an indeterminate place and trust that GOD's plan for my life was the only option. Yes, my pride took a hit but for the first time since I could remember, I felt a wave of peace and assurance.

Given this place, I was able to make good on the main promise made to my Mom. And, in August 2015, the church purchased a building to call home. I was feeling accomplished spiritually– however financially I was in a crisis. Money was short, bills were piling up, collectors were calling, and my credit was becoming damaged. I had entered into a place where I began to ask GOD for provision. I asked Him to open a door so that I could get caught up on my bills and live more comfortably. Well, He did just that. I was recruited back into Corporate America to oversee a merger. Once again, I found myself accepting one of those "Impossible" type positions. This time I was more prepared and kind of hyped to see if I still had "it", after a two-year sabbatical.

Chapter 4

Well, here we go again. I am now about 1.5 years in, and I start feeling that itch to advance. At that time, I was succeeding as the Operations Manager and was managing being a Pastor pretty well. Then it happened; a position for the VP of Operations was posted. Obviously, I began to inquire and then was endorsed to apply by the resigning VP and the President of the Company. In all of this, I still keep praying and asking GOD to lead and direct me. As the interview process convened, I took ill and was hospitalized for a short period of time. Even through this minor setback, I still was motivated and quickly returned to work. Once I returned, I kept in stride with the long arduous hiring process and ended up making it to the Finals.

During the Final phase, I was interviewed by the Chief Operations Officer. Now peep this: At the conclusion of the interview, he gets up and kneels on one knee and kisses my hand. He said and I quote, "In my yesteryears I was a Litigator. If I had you on my team, I would have never lost a case." He then gets up and writes my salary on a piece of paper and says, "This is where we will start you." OMG!!!! Tears streamed down my face as I began to praise GOD for this awesome opportunity.

The next day, I'm called into the President's office and was told they went with the other candidate. To appease my disappointment, they gave my raise (nowhere near what I would have been making). At any rate, through my utter disgust – I quickly came to terms that the elected candidate must be someone spectacular, and maybe I could be pushed to another level, under their tutelage. Well, at the introduction reception, here walks in this Less Experienced, Unpolished, and No-Degree having White Blond!! It was definitely a déjà vu moment. I literally thought I was BEING PUNKED????

So again, I found myself drawing back to God for some answers. In short, HE revealed that HE could not trust me to focus on Destiny along with Corporate Advancement. He knew that this type of promotion would have taken me even further out my ALIGNMENT with HIS Will. He then concluded by telling me to prepare for my resignation...OUCH!

Conclusion

The following summer as I was preparing to go into work, I heard God gently say, "Put in your notice." I obeyed HIS voice. I went in, gave my notice. This sent shock waves throughout the company. No one could believe I was just willing to walk away. You see this leap; unlike the first one did not come with any severance or unemployment. All financial ties were cut immediately. I was figuratively launching away from the familiar and into the DEEP.

The lessons learned through this experience is closely related to the story in the Bible where Peter, an experienced fisherman could not catch fish. He could not catch fish until Jesus entered the ship and charged him to leave the familiar and launch out further.

Luke 5 records this story and there are three key nuggets that have lifted me during this perpetual walk of FAITH. First, not all rejection is bad. Divine Rejection will place you in the presence of Jesus and change the rules of engagement. The objective is to become more focused on HIM than your dilemma. Matthew 6:33, tells us to seek FIRST the Kingdom of God and then the things that we desire will be added. I, like Peter, had to understand that my rejection was repurposed to push me closer to Jesus and thereby aligning me with my Destiny. Second, the familiar can be crippling. Peter used his expertise to attempt to fish. With all his years and experience – he resulted in catching nothing. Sometimes we become very robotic and comfortable in dealing with the matters of life. It is easy to utilize the concepts and ideals that have proven reliable in the past. However, eventually in order to GROW, one must be aware of their surroundings and discern when there is a need to make adjustments.

Lastly, obedience creates a space for contagious elevation. Once Jesus stepped on the boat and advised Peter to launch out deeper, Peter had to go alone and left the other boat behind. While in the deep he let down his nets and the number of fish was too great for him to handle. It was at that time the other boat was beckoned to come help handle the INCREASE. When we are strategically placed and operating in Divine Order, our obedience will have a rippling effect to everything connected to us. It steps full throttle into the Biblical concept of Overflow. Once our nets are full – God will use our access to bless others.

The theme of my story is going from Aspiration to Alignment. With all of my Aspirations, I remained unfilled until I Aligned with God's Will for my life. I can honestly say that I feel free and more determined to complete the Assignments that God has for me. I KNOW that I am called to preach the unadulterated WORD OF GOD. I KNOW that I have been called to serve the community through the gifts of Compassion and Love. I KNOW that I am called to help uplift and encourage people to TRUST GOD through the toughest of times. I KNOW I am called to give voice and advocacy to those that feel invisible and/or dismissed. Lastly, I KNOW that as everything continues to evolve, so should my hunger and thirst to KNOW more.

I often revisit the conversation with my Mother about getting "it". Oddly, she never told me what "it" was – just that I would know "it" once I truly got "it". Well, I can testify that I started to get "it" a few months after my 25th birthday. And "it" has been an enlightening journey. And, while I will not spoil and tell you what "it" is I'll just say take her advice and go get "it" for yourself. "It" will be worth it.

END

Finding Purpose through Pain

by Kim Rivera

Hello precious reader. From the time we are created, God has great plans for us. However, we tend to go through trials, disappointments, setbacks, failures, hurts, pains, consequences, some self-inflicted and some by others. It's a part of life. Through it all, God is with us giving us strength and preparing us for our future as we submit our lives to him. Let me explain. My name is Kim Rivera and I have been through divorce, abandonment, physical abuse, betrayal, rejection, and I am a cancer survivor. I grew up in and around Pittsburgh, PA. I grew up in church knowing the way of Christianity. I come from a basically normal family structure where we laughed a lot.

My parents separated and divorced when I was about 12 years old. When I was about 19, I became rebellious to the ways I was taught in Christianity. I became promiscuous and partied a lot. I was able to maintain a job after graduating from school as a licensed nurse. I went through several boyfriends who had lied, cheated, and at times were physically abusive. I am not putting all the blame on them; I caused some things by making many mistakes and bad decisions. I even went through married men in the church who were trying to get with me, but I never submitted to that. I considered married men off limits. But I grew hatred towards them. I developed some low self-esteem, distrust, anger, resentment, paranoia, jealousy, bitterness and unforgiveness. Some of these emotions got incorporated in my character, and I was making decisions from broken areas in my soul. At the age of 25, I left everything behind and enlisted in the army, trying to run away from my past. Little did I know, I was still carrying it along with me and taking it into other relationships. The military was one of the best things that happened to me. I learn a lot of discipline in some areas of my life. I traveled to other states and countries; I spent about 18 months in Germany. I met my future husband there; he was from Turkey; we married about a year after we met. I was so infatuated with him that I ignored all the warning signs. Little did I know; I believe he wanted to get married just to get to the United States. Two years after we came to the United States, his behavior started changing toward me. We were stationed on Fort Dix. At that time, I rededicated my life back to the Lord: and our relationship continued to grow apart. He was Muslim, and I tried to do all I could to make it work but made so many mistakes. After I timed out of the military, I obtained a Federal employee position working for General Services Administration, and he obtained a good truck driving job.

Then the lying, cheating and financial irresponsibility started. Another year went by, and he totally abandoned me and my son. I was devastated. Thank God for my job; however, it was not enough to pay all the bills. Also, I was in a church of caring believers who helped me along the way. I received very little help from him financially after that point. The state of New Jersey had to make him give me finances; however, most of the time they could not find him. Three months after he left, I developed a cancerous growth in my parotid gland. It was taken out, so they prepared more for radiation. I was only 32 years old at the time. I felt numb like I was in a movie. At that point, I did not want to live anymore; I stopped eating regular meals and got so skinny. My thought was that I had to live for my son. I became angry with God: How could you allow this to happen? I discovered later it was not what God was doing to me; it was what he was doing for and in me. My family was about six hours away, visiting sometime; however, God became my source.

For the next 15 years, I learned to trust God and my Christian life grew in leaps and bounds. It was not easy and many times I made mistakes, but I did not stay down; I repented and got back up. God help me to persevere. I asked God to reveal what was going on down on the inside of me. He did just that. I discovered I was still suffering emotional trauma and carrying a lot of my past that was hindering my future. I made a decision to get free. Through study of God's word, other biblical books, prayer, and godly men and women, I received physical and emotional healing and deliverance. It was a process, and I am still maintaining to stay free. I went to bible school, where I earned my bachelor's in theological studies. I had a strong desire to marry again. I was on the hunt and made more mistakes; however, I did not stay down for the count. I went back to school again for a refresher for a licensed practical nurse and worked a part time job on the weekends to supplement my income.

After some years went by, I decided there is no man out there for me, so I focused more on my son and my relationship with God. God did so many miracles: healing, unexpected big child support checks, bonuses from my job, promotions and so much more. God even sent an angel to help me. One moment he was there, and the next he was gone. I became a licensed minister and did a lot of outreach in hospitals, prisons, streets and drug rehabs and after school youth programs. I was so focused on doing God's work. I loved it. Little did I know; there was a widower at our church that was watching me. He was a minister also. We dated a few times, and I knew he was the one. We were married about 18 months later.

After that I continued to grow even more in the Lord. My husband helped nurture and brought out spiritual gifts that I did not know I had. We went to school of the spirit together and many other biblical classes. I obtained Certification as a life coach and life skills instructor. In 2008, we were both commissioned and ordained as Pastors. I taught in the very school I attended above on inner healing. I obtained several more promotions on my job and retired early at the age of 54. I wrote a book in 2016 called "Will the real you please stand up, Getting beyond your past". All the experiences I went through and the lessons I learned helped me write my book. Some aspects I learn through all these experiences are (1). Use failures as leverage to start over again more intelligently. (2). God sometimes uses rejection as a tool for direction that helps us discover his divine intention. (3) God has an impeccable way of developing purpose through pain. I leave you with this scripture. Proverbs 24:16 for a just man falls seven times; and rises up again.

END

BLESSINGS

Faith is the strongest known driving force in the lives of the majority of Black women. Historically speaking, Black churches began to form in the early eighteenth century. Since then, Black churches have been a cornerstone in the Black community and not just for weddings or funerals and church on Sundays. Churches in the Black community have been educational and safe havens. During the time of American slavery, Black churches were known to be held on plantations. Moving through time, Black churches began to relocate depending on circumstances, and at times runaway slaves could hide out in the lower level of churches. By the civil rights movement in the mid 1950's, Black churches all over America became yet again the home of civil rights activists traveling in from out of town.

It has been found that Black women represent an estimated 66-88% of the church population (Barnes, 2006). Despite the fact that men still hold the majority of the leadership roles. Black women are said to be the backbone of the church. The prayers of the mothers of the church have had an historical astronomical effect on the lives of entire generations. The power behind a Black women's prayer is unmatched. Since the beginning of time, Black women from every generation have proven that their faith in God has been the reason for their strength to overcome such pain and tragedy, including women like Harriet Tubman who listened to God's voice to follow the North Star. She was willing to put her faith in God, and trust that He would see her through.

Nevertheless, there might not have been a Sojourner Truth without a Harriet Tubman. These two women's prayers and faith in God opened the doors for Dina B. Wells-Barnett, Dorothy Height, Daisy Bates, Ella Baker, Barbara Jordan, and Coretta Scott King. A Black woman who stands firm on Psalm 46.5, "God is within her, she will not fall." Why would they fear? Black women's pain and sorrow never got left by the wayside; God was always listening. Generations of God-fearing Black women got down on their knees and prayed for better days. The obedience to God she exhibits has been a covering over many entire communities and generations. Black women have listened to God's call through their lives, and that has been one of the reasons He has used us to be the strength of the family and the glue to keep things together. In many cases, the Black woman is the head of the household and she goes to God on everything. The strength of a Black woman comes from Jesus, make no mistake about it; it is his grace and mercy that fills Black women up to press on. "God is within her; she shall not be moved God will help her at dawn." (Psalm 46:5)

God's Grace Brought Me Through

by Elnora Poole

I was the baby of the family and the first out of 11 children to graduate from high school, class of 1964. I loved school and graduated 13th out of 133. That made my momma so proud, prouder than words could explain. You see, momma couldn't read or write, and she never went to school. So, education meant a lot to her for me to surpass the stereotype of being an uneducated Black woman. Back in those days school hadn't integrated yet. I graduated two years before *"Board vs. Brown."*

Nobody ever picked on me in school because they knew if they did, my brothers would get them. I would get on the bus, and I would make sure I sat next to the Valedictorians, class officers and all of the prestigious students who got straight A's. The ride to school was about one hour long, and at home I didn't have anyone to help me with my homework, so this was the perfect opportunity to learn all I could. My passion was theatre and drama. In the first play I ever did, which was at Union Hall, I played the role of a policeman. While on stage, I began feeling my pants falling down, so I grabbed the side and took the play gun out and ad libbed saying, "Hold It." Then the whole crowd went crazy!

After that, I was in more plays as a nosy old woman, and I became famous in town for my comical stage presence. My drama teacher Ms. Stick said I have enough talent to get into college on a drama scholarship. The sad truth was that I knew I couldn't leave momma home by herself, not after all she did for me. My siblings were all grown and doing their own thing and I felt it was my responsibility to step up and look after momma. So, I decided to turn down my dreams of becoming an actress and movie star.

As I got off the bus one day, I looked up and saw my boyfriend's little sister Lois strutting in a sweater I gave to Isaac. She wanted to make sure I saw it too, and I couldn't wait to confront him. Isaac was five years older than me, so we didn't go to high school together.

10th grade in high school was a struggle. My brother Poppa was shot and killed, and my other brother Roy was shot. That was a real hard time, because I didn't know what I was going to do. Poppa was a provider and would always get me the new records. It was during the wake for my brother poppa that I locked eyes with a handsome young man with the most beautiful smile. Still in my heart to this day, I feel it was love at first sight; we started dating.

My boyfriend asked me to be my date to the prom, and my heart melted, but I couldn't let him know because all the girls liked him. For my 11th grade prom, I wore a White sleeveless gown and a shawl, with a blue corsage. While all the other kids could stay out all night after, I wasn't allowed. We went out on the town with some friends for an hour or two after prom; however, I had to be home by midnight. As we pulled into the driveway, it never failed; my momma's eyes would be peeking through the bedroom window. If I took too long to come in the house, she would open the front door. Even on date nights she would make sure we stayed in the living room, it was still fun playing our records and gazing into each other's eyes. But as soon as 10 pm hit, she would bust in the room and say, "You know what time it is."

In 12th grade, my girls Tiny Lee and Carol, and I got into a car and snuck into a juke joint. As soon as we set foot in that trashy place, somebody from the church recognized us, but it was too late. The next morning at church, all the women knew, and Ms. Pearl was busy telling my momma how she heard this and that. Following this my mother said, "If you lie, you steal and if you steal, you'll lie, and nobody will believe you." I stole an Apple once, and when I made it home, she made me turn all the way back and return it. She was known for her honesty and her faith in God.

For 12th grade prom, Isaac and I had broken up, so I didn't have a date. Meanwhile, he was still busy trying to figure out who I was going to go with. Every chance his little sister Lois got, she told him lies about who I might be going with. It wasn't until my cousin Lenard asked me if he could take me because he had already graduated and wanted to talk to a girl at the prom that I finally had a date. So, I said "Sure you can take me, as long as you buy the corsage and whatever I want to eat after". After the prom was over, we all were leaving. In the parking lot stood Isaac with a group of guys drinking and trying to be nosy and see who was with whom. But I wasn't worried about it; I just kept walking. Then a few short months later, he went back into service (military).

During this time, I met Orlando Carter, a pretty boy who drove a smooth 1964 Ford Hatchback. He was a slick talker who wanted to buy materialistic things. So, at the time he bought me a huge birthstone. Claude Beckom, the handsome roughneck type with the smooth low rider wanted to date me; I had to tell him I was engaged. So, he moved on and let me be.

Then one day my mom said to me, "Elizabeth, you engaged to get married to Isaac who seems to be a nice young man. So, what you have these other niggas coming by here fo? Don't be playin with people's hearts."

Six months later we ran into each other again at the fair and my cousin Curley was with me drooling over Isaac. Then he asked to walk with me and talk, so we did, and he expressed his interest in me. He exclaimed that we should get married. So, on July 16, 1966, we eloped because he had to go back to war. We went to a courthouse in Virginia. I lied to my mother and told her I was going to a friend's house nearby. When he went to Korea, I was always running to and from the mailbox for love letters we would send to each other.

In October, we had the traditional wedding ceremony. It was the first wedding at Union Hall Baptist Church Danville Virginia. My father wouldn't give any of his daughters away. When my soon to be husband at the time confronted my father to ask for my hand, my father said "I ain't got a damn thing to give away." That's just the kind of man my father was, very blunt and straightforward. He said what he meant and meant what he said, although he did give a lot of hams and other meats for the wedding. He never went to the church house regardless of the fact his father Bob gave the land where the church was built on. So, my brother Roy walked me down the aisle. I had the traditional bridal party with a ring bearer and the most adorable flower girls. Then there I was staring at my groom, but nobody knew we were already married.

After the traditional wedding, he went back to Colorado for a month. Then, he was off to Fort Knox Army in Kentucky. I went back home and stayed with my mom after that because he got orders to go to Vietnam. While this all was taking place in 1969, there was a fire at my mother's house, and we lost everything. High school yearbooks, Christmas ornaments, family photo albums, all of my wedding pictures and more were forever gone. Back in those days the old folk didn't believe in insurance.

After the fire, my mom and brother Eliete went to stay with one of my other sisters Riata. My husband came home from Vietnam, and he had orders for Fort Story Virginia Beach. He got quarters on the military base which was military housing.

Then in 1970, I went to the doctors and was trying to find out why I couldn't get pregnant, and the doctor said, "Mrs. Poole you are pregnant." That was such an exciting moment for me and my husband. I was so excited to put on those little soon to be mommy tops. After having lived in Virginia Beach for four years we got orders to Germany. I refuse to leave my family in Virginia, so my husband went without me. That was a rough time in my life. If I didn't know Jesus, I wouldn't have made it through. My beautiful mother-in-law kept me encouraged and would always tell me, "Don't listen to those people out there trying to bring you down baby."

Then, next thing I knew my husband came home and I was pregnant again with my next child, another baby boy. This was a happy time, until the tragic loss of my father in 1971. Soon after the birth of my second child we moved to New Jersey. My husband got orders to Fort Dix, New Jersey. We lived on the military base for two years, as the years passed, he got orders to Germany. While he was away in Germany, I went back home to stay in Virginia with momma. After six months, it was over in Germany my husband got sick and got sent to Walter Reed Hospital in

Washington DC. Then when he recovered, he got orders again to go back to New Jersey, so I went on and I followed him with our two boys.

On February 5, 1977 on a cold rough day, we bought our first home in New Jersey. This is a moment that I'll never forget, the excitement of having my very own first home with my lovely husband and two children. I couldn't wait to dress up my kitchen living room and front yard. For the first year we struggled not being able to afford furniture for the living room, but we still enjoyed every moment of having our own. My flowers were my recreation time. I spent many days in my flower garden, I took pride in seeing them grow.

In 1977, I got blood clots in my lungs and I was in the hospital for 32 days. During that time, nobody thought I would make it. The doctors thought that was gonna be it, and if I hadn't had the Lord and the church family, I would have made it. I found out what true Christians were, and being so far from home it was a blessing to have the nearby families who stepped in. The Thompson family stepped in to take care of my two children. My husband was working a lot when he wasn't at the hospital. I wanted to come home so bad for my children. So, I would lie to the doctors and say I was okay. Then the doctor let me go once and no later than I got home, I had to turn right back and go to the hospital again. I wasn't fully recovered. For about six months I was on a blood thinner. Then after some time had passed, I really recovered, and I was released.

In 1981, I thought I had a tumor but soon found out I was with a child again. It was my best pregnancy; I worked up until Christmas. I remember at work they didn't even want me to touch a piece of paper. I thought finally God would bless me and my husband with a beautiful little girl. Back then there weren't any fancy reveal parties and doctors said it's a 50/50 chance. On February 17, 1982, I gave birth to another boy. My baby was 8 pounds and 12 ounces. My husband retired from the military after serving 23 years in the army and soon after he worked at a prison for a year and soon after that he got a good job at the post office. Through the years I worked several jobs but in 1986, I landed a job that I would keep for 18 years. Working at the mess hall on base as a cook was something I took pride in. I've always been admired for my cooking, especially how I would be able to cook for over 2,000 soldiers. They all would scuffle and push to get a plate of my down-home cooking.

In 1990, my husband and I were blessed to kickstart our third generation. We finally were blessed with our first grandchild, a beautiful baby girl. At last, my husband and I had the chance to enjoy a little girl; we finally could buy pretty pink dresses and furry teddy bears. During the joyful years of being grandparents, my husband was hospitalized, and the happy year came to a screeching halt. No one will ever understand the devastating feeling I felt when the doctors told me my husband had (Asian orange) he also contracted cancer in one of his lungs. After time and time again, we were denied financial support from the military. So, I called Washington, DC and I would say, "I want to speak to the president." I was inviting the Veterans Administration (VA) to come visit a dying man. I witness watching my husband cough up blood. Our youngest son was 12 years old, and my husband tried to get in as much quality time as he could. I would look out and see him teaching him how to drive at 12. Then next thing, I knew he would be taking him fishing.

On August 12, 1994 at 3:45 pm, my only love, Isaac Poole, took his last breath. I still remember hopping in my little blue Toyota to go home and take a quick shower and come right back. Before I could get back, he was gone. 26 days later, I was blessed with a new addition to the family, another grandchild, a beautiful little girl. After his death, I spent a lot of my time with my grandchildren, working, and catching as many church services as possible. I would never be home for long if I wasn't at church or work, I would be flying back and forth from New Jersey to Virginia to spend time with my siblings back home.

It was a normal day at the mess hall, and I was helping a co-worker of mine with picking lobsters out of freezing cold water. In 2002, my health took the most painful spiral down. I got frostbite in my right hand. That night I remember my fingers turning Black. So, I rushed to the hospital and the doctor said, "OH BOY! YOU'VE GOT FROSTBITE! BUT YOU'RE BLESSED, MS. POOLE BECAUSE YOU STILL HAVE FEELING IN YOUR HAND." The pain was so excruciating that I told the doctors they could just cut my hand off. That was the start of my diabetes gone all out of control. Before this I would take one pill a day and I would walk the track. Since that day I have had a rollercoaster of health issues start: diabetes, high blood pressure, lung problems, and a defibrillator for my heart because I have congestive heart failure. I currently attend dialysis three times a week for my kidneys. And I'm an anemic who is on Coumadin, which is a blood thinner. Through God's grace, I'm able to wake up every day and enjoy the life that I have the best way I can with my family and loved ones still left in Virginia.

At this point in my life, I reminisce on my past and how God wouldn't bring me as far to leave me. I always believed in God since I was 11 years old when on a stormy Wednesday night, I went with my aunt to revival, and I never turned back. I still remember I gave my pastor my hand, and I gave God my heart. And through it all I've been rolling with him since, and he's never let me down. When I was a little girl at that revival, I was determined I was gonna join the church. So, mama wouldn't have to keep telling me to sit down when I was shouting in church. As a teenager I enjoy church more than I enjoyed the clubs and going out dancing and stuff. I always got along with the elderly more than I got along with my own peers, calling myself "an antique." I told myself after I got frostbite that I just have to keep pressing on and see what the end is going to be with Jesus holding my hand. Growing up I will listen to my mother in the other room praying before bed and I never really understood the words that she was saying, but now there's a girl in my faith in the years that have gone by and I know what she meant.

Through the years, I have had great friends, pastors, and family. The greatest foundation of all was my Lord and Savior Jesus Christ, when no one else would answer the phone, I could just call on him. When people ask me who I am the first child of God, I'm a wife forever, I'm a mother of three great sons, I'm a grandmother of five grandchildren, and I'm a great grandmother of two beautiful children.

To my husband I will always love you and not a day goes by that I don't think about you.

To my mother, I love you, and I can't thank you enough for all you did for me. I always knew you were praying hard for me.

To my three sons: please love one another, and even when I'm gone, look after each other, and you'll be blessed.

To my granddaughters I love you all with all my heart, and I'm very proud of you. Continue to keep your values and never lose sight of them, because if you do you lose everything. And continue to strive and your dreams will come true; you see how far God has brought you because of your faith. Please keep that up.

To my grandsons I love you very much. I'm very proud of you; I want so much for you. And one I think is on the right track and the other is not, but I'm always praying for you.

To my great grandchildren you are my little queen and king. I love them with all my heart. They can do no wrong; they are so precious. Keep it up.

To my only living sibling: My beautiful sister, may God continue to bless you; I love you.

RELATIONSHIPS

Mamie Till mourns the death of her son Emmett

Black mothers who have sons come to a nightmarish reality that every day when your son leaves the house, he might be killed. This frightening truth has caused Black mothers all across America to grieve and be fearful of their sons' lives every day. Black mothers throughout American history have had to deal with being trapped in what some may call a double bind of racism, meaning that many Black mothers having grown up in a society filled with racial profiling and police misconduct against Black people, and now their young Black male sons are targeted at earlier ages and killed viciously.

Throughout history and still today, Black mothers are traumatized by the pain of having to bury their sons as a result of America's racism. Time and time again, Black mothers tragically are left with painful and tragic bonds due to systemic racism that keeps taking the lives of their sons. So many Black mothers share the searing painful tears of losing a child. From Emmitt Till (1955) to Trayvon Martin (2012) to Tamir Rice (2014) to Eric Gardener (2014), and fast forward just a few short years. Here, Black mothers are still facing the loss of their sons: Antwon Rose II (2018) and George Floyd (2020). Black mothers like Tamika Palmer who have daughters face this same heart wrenching truth. The loss of 26-year-old Breonna

Taylor brought forth the reality that Black girls and boys both have targets on their backs every day they wake up. Justice is long overdue. Black mothers continue to fight for change, and because of these tragedies, so many Black mothers are talking with their sons and daughters regarding the timeline of truth they are up against.

Blindfolded Sight

Blue and foggy red flashing lights flickering in my rearview mirror

6 o'clock news replaying in my mind

Another cop shot and killed another young Black...

Mother, Father, Child, Pastor, Student, Athlete

Heart wrenching nightmare possibilities running through my mind untamed

All of the "what if's and could be's"

My bravery gave up and unlocked my caged fears

As a coat of tears began to blur my vision

My heart swallowed whole by rapid beats

NO LIFE LINE

911! HELL NO THEY DIRTY TOO

That inner fire tried to push away my tears that piled behind my eyelids

Fears faced me vs. me facing my fears

Footstep vibrations coming towards me

Only steps away last breaths to take

"License and registration" Officer say

Time choked my oxygen making each breath impossible to take

Bloody possibilities shook my soul

Taught thought hit me

Don't make this car your casket

WE RISE

"Get home now" Officer said

NO GOODNIGHT

NO EXPLANATION

Relief raised my spirit

God's grace covered me

A relieved peace chilled my body slowly

"What's the big fuss, it's only the police" Says the rest of the world

Who will never see what divides us?

"Voice Beneath the Surface "

By Jasmine Poole

FATHERS & DAUGHTERS

Malcolm X and Muhammad Ali with children

The first man a girl should ever love is her father. The most important relationship is the one between a person and God. Although that is a true statement, God did not make man/woman to be alone. Relationships serve a heavy purpose in the molding of a person's life. The relationship between father and daughter is one of the most important relationships between a young girl and a man. Father-daughter relationships vary depending on the family. Although Black fathers take a bad rap for being absent from their child's life, many young Black girls are blessed with a father they know and have a relationship with. There is just something so special about having the opportunity to witness a Black man with his daughter. That bond is unbreakable and special in more ways than one.

A positive relationship between a father and his daughter can have a magnificent impact on both of their lives. The power of a healthy relationship

73

between a father and his daughter can even determine whether or not she develops into a strong, confident woman. Little girls learn how to be treated by a man by the first man they come in contact with. So, if the man is a gentleman and treats her with respect; that is what she will be most acceptable to later on in life. On the other end of things, if the father is not a positive role model in his daughter's life, this can cause serious damage to her future encounters with men. The power of a father's influence in his little girl's life shapes her self-esteem, self-image, confidence and opinions of men.

A father plays a necessary role in a little girl's life. Innumerable times, fathers might miss out on the necessary moments she needs in order to not accept just any man later on in life. Frequently conversations revolve around the significance between a father and his son. Interestingly, teenage girls who have healthy relationships with their fathers are two times less likely to get pregnant as a teenager. Less likely to be in a domestic violence relationship, *"Slap! His hard palm came across my cheek with quick intensity. I heard bells in my head and the living room swam around me, as I crumpled to the floor. When I opened my eyes, he was standing over me, looking down at me. "Get Up," he said and stepped out of my blurry vision. I couldn't move, my face was on fire, and my hot tears only stung more."* (McFadden. 2002)

The well fathered daughter is also more likely to achieve educational goals. The consequence of being a poorly fathered daughter she is more likely to develop clinical depression, along with other health issues such as eating disorders. Almost every person reading this has heard the saying, "Any man can make a baby, but a real man takes care of his child." This still stands firm on solid truth. A father's involvement in his daughter's life can potentially determine her life forever. When a young woman falls in love the majority of the time, she attracts similar characteristics that make up those of her father, despite whether they are good or bad. She sees her father in most men because she has been so accustomed to his behaviors and habits. Another example of this is in the story, Warmest December, *"Hy-Lo was with me even though he was miles and miles away. He came in different skin colors, read the Bible or just the sports page. I noticed him no matter what disguise he wore."* *(McFadden. 2002)*Every little girl needs her father to teach, love, and protect her. The relationship between a father and his daughter is more important than it gets credit for.

"We need you"

It's Okay Not to be Okay;
Victory Over Stigma

by Rochelle Graham, LPC

As a young girl raised by a single mother, I often struggled with my identity and feelings of unworthiness, as most little girls without fathers do. I grew up as an only child with a military mom, who occasionally brought her work home. There was little to no time for hugs, bedtime stories, and sweet cupcake kisses. I was her 'little soldier' and showing any kind of emotion besides happiness was almost a sin. I was constantly reminded that even though I lacked the influence of a supportive father figure, I had better be grateful to be able to attend a "good school", live in the suburbs, and have a mom who can afford anything else I wanted. Everything on the surface appeared normal and good.

As a teenager I worked in the mall and had quite a social life. Everything about my life appeared "normal." Under the surface I felt trapped as I struggled with sexual promiscuity, codependency, depression, and anxiety. In December 2000 at 6 a.m., I found myself in the women's clinic planning to terminate my first pregnancy. I remember feeling numb. I wanted so much to feel validated by men that I didn't mind getting pregnant just so I could have a man say those three words I haven't heard from my father or mother which was, "I love you." I terminated two more pregnancies after that from later relationships. It was like a pattern for me from the ages of seventeen to twenty-one, just for the sake of feeling validated or worthy to someone. It wasn't until my senior year in college that I started to reflect and take a deeper look at myself, and suddenly I realized that I was not okay.

When I graduated from college, I was young, single, and free, and so what could possibly be wrong? I tried to hide my sadness for so long that I was convinced that nothing was wrong. My estranged relationship with my father and his family made me feel neglected and unwanted. The times that I tried to reach out to him unsuccessfully went unnoticed, and I felt like I wasn't good enough for anything. During this time, I couldn't count on any emotional support from the maternal side of my family. I knew emotional support didn't exist in that direction; it never has. During this time, I felt overwhelmed with intense emotions and didn't know what to do with them. I decided to leave New Jersey and move to St. Louis, Missouri with my boyfriend at the time. I was questioned and berated for "shackin up" with a man. However, many people didn't understand that moving to Missouri was a way for me to leave toxicity behind. I was told that my boyfriend and I living together would lead to a disastrous relationship and that I would regret it for the rest of my life.

When I moved to Missouri, I enrolled in a master's Program at Lindenwood University and four years later graduated with a degree in Counseling. I stayed in Missouri for five years, during which I have found my identity, what I will accept, and what I refuse to accept in my life. I like to call my time spent in Missouri my "wilderness". Throughout one's lifespan there is a moment in time when you have to go through a time of self-discovery, and sometimes that means leaving your home or comfort zone. I discovered who I am and my capabilities, and I began reaching my full potential. I began to build a deeper relationship with God and realized that He was the only Father that I needed to be validated by. Understanding this has helped me become more confident in knowing that I am worthy of being loved.

When I received my master's in counseling, I vowed to help those young women who like myself have been taught to suppress their true feelings. I want to spread the message for the rest of my life that it's okay not to be okay. I understand what it feels like to be silenced because people may not understand or may even disregard your struggles. I understand what it must feel like for people to be dismissive of feelings and disregard emotions. Currently, I am a licensed therapist (LPC) dedicated to helping youth who struggle with father absenteeism, depression, and anxiety. I used to feel hopeless and unwanted because I knew I would never be anyone's little princess. *Little girls need their fathers*, but I wasn't blessed in that way. However, I turned my pain into progress and broke some of the generational curses that tried to destroy my spirit. As a licensed therapist, author, mother of four, and wife to an amazing husband and father, I found my voice, and I have dedicated my life to helping others find their voices too. I may have never been daddy's little princess, but by God's grace and mercy, I turned tragedy into triumph and became a Queen.

END

HER LOVE

Coretta Scott King and the Rev. Dr. Martin Luther King, Jr.

How can you love someone else if you don't love yourself? That brings me to the so-called "Angry Black Women". Many people in the world like to portray black women as angry and emotional. Millions of dollars have been made off of the tears and heartbreak of Black women. We as black women have to snatch the pen from Hollywood and tell our own love stories, because true love does exist for Black women. One example of the pain and sorrow which lead to true happiness was in the classic movie *Waiting to Exhale*. There is a scene in the movie that perfectly captures falsified depictions of the emotions of a Black woman's love. In it, Bernadine Harris, one of the main characters, played by the beautiful and talented Angela Bassett, is told by her Black husband and father of their two children that their marriage is over, and to top it off, he is leaving her for a White woman. Fast forward to the infamous angry Black woman scene when Bernadine has had enough and grabs her soon to be ex-husband's clothes and sets them on fire in the car outside. This scene, just like many other scenes in this classic motion picture, reveals the true pain felt by so many Black women. Many times, as black women, we live the majority of our lives single or alone. So often black women hear black men say, "I'm gonna find me a white woman who will treat a brotha good" or "Black women are not attractive to me". (Sidenote: WHAT IS YOUR MOTHER?) Most of those same men who have the audacity to tell a black queen she is not attractive were born by a woman just like the women he calls unattractive. History shows that this thought process was taught to the black man over time. "She was considered less than a woman. She was a cross between a whore and a workhorse. Black men internalized the white man's opinion of Black women. And, if you ask me, a lot of us still act like we're back on the plantation with massa pulling the strings." (Assata Shakur, 1987)

Black women are constantly labeled with being too independent, or angry and bitter. "When I asked why, they said white women are sweeter. Black women are evil; white women are more understanding, Black women are more demanding" but these emotions stem from the reality we as black women have had to go through. (Assata 112) There are many reasons behind our singleness stigma; one in particular is "patience". We are extremely impatient, "Sometimes I just want to cry because so many of God's girls are impatient settling." (Kendall, 1995) Being single in this day and age is extremely difficult to accept. Everywhere you look, whether that be on social media and see all the beautiful couples in love or you turn on the television. Love is all over; instead of being jealous, just be patient.

Single

It is extremely important that we as women fully understand the process of finding our soulmate and being properly equipped for when that time comes. These are the ways to prepare before finding true love.

1. Pray. God needs to be the foundation of any relationship. So, make sure you check in with God daily. This doesn't mean praying for Him to send your true love like an amazon package in two to three days. This means wait and pray that He will reveal your true love when the time is right. As you go to God in prayer be sure

to stop and listen for His voice. Oftentimes we go to God in prayer, but it is more putting in request after request and less seeking His face. So, stop and learn to recognize His voice.

2. Journal the journey. The power of writing down your inner thoughts and feelings can serve as fuel to keep going. When you start feeling down and discouraged that you'll never find that special someone, go back and take a look at how far you have come. Then keep moving forward. It's okay to look back but its not okay to go back. Journaling your thoughts is a form of therapy that helps heal old wounds and lead to growth.

3. Forgive your past. The only way to truly move on and prepare your heart for your true love is by forgiving your past pain and the person who left you scarred. The forgiveness is not for them; it's for you. This sometimes calls for reaching out to someone who hurt you and making peace with them. Forgiveness is powerful. Even though the person who hurt you might not deserve forgiveness its best that you forgive that person because until you do God may not open the door to your next chapter.

4. The power of a circle: Good God -fearing friends who genuinely love and care about you are very hard to find, but it is not impossible. "When a woman stops growing spiritually, the lack of progress can often be traced back to a friendship that undermined her commitment to Jesus." (Kendall, 1995) This power friendship alliance can also be referred to as the support circle which will keep you accountable. The support circle can consist of friends, loved ones, therapists, or your pastor. It is key that you meet with them regularly and conduct your meetings on the following: total honesty, constructive criticism, and no judgement. They'll help keep you on track when trying to remain grounded.

5. Set goals. Give yourself a timeframe to grow as a single individual. So often God wants to use this single moment in your life to elevate you with no distractions. Here are some ideas while you wait on God to send the love of your life:

Grow spiritually

Exercise & get healthy

Further your education

Focus on your career

Start the business you've been talking about

Travel

Once your priorities are all in line, you will begin to be complete but remain patient and continue to seek God. Keep in mind single women reading this that just because you have completed all of the elements towards strengthening oneself doesn't mean your dream spouse will be at your front door tomorrow. So, stay focused and keep praying and working on being the best you possible.

Dating

For those of you who are dating, this stage does not mean you've reached the finish line. This is only the beginning. Remember that no man will ever complete you, no matter how real the love is between the both of you, "Incompleteness is not the result of being single, but of not being full of Jesus." (Kendall, 1995) The only one who can complete you is Jesus. So, step into a new relationship already complete, so you both compliment one another. "A woman was not created to complete a man but to compliment a man." (Gen.2:18) Black love is absolutely beautiful but so are all forms of love. As Black women we so often feel as if we are betraying the Black man if we date outside our race. That is not true. Who's to say that your true love isn't of a different race? So, remain open to date all different races. So often, we as women during the dating faze get caught feeling with the pressure of having to be intimate with the man to keep him. So many women tell themselves, if I don't sleep with him, he will leave me, well let him leave. Some women spend years in and out of relationships because they simply haven't learned their worth. If this is you, stop and start over. This might mean deleting toxic ex's you might still have a tendency to go back to because its comfortable. Or deleting all the men from your online dating app. Waiting to find that special someone can be filled with ups and downs. Dating means opening up to new people and figuring out if there is chemistry between you both. It helps to just trust God and keep a positive mindset along the journey to finding your true love. Some other advice while dating would be to ask yourself specific questions such as:

What characteristics do I want in my future husband?

What do I deserve?

What relationship patterns do I need to break?

Marriage

Be sure to go about this process the same way you'd go looking at a house for sale. Meaning take time to pray and ask God for confirmation before saying "I do". Above anything you both have to make sure the foundation which is God is strong. Keep in mind that marriage shouldn't go into unhealed scars and secrets. It is extremely pivotal to let the love of your life know all your weaknesses. This is sort of like leaving your baggage at the door before entering into your new house (marriage). There are some things married couples should try these consists of the following:

Spiritual Counseling

Many times, married couples expect their spouses to change because they're married. This couldn't be further from the truth. You can't change someone, even the person you have committed yourself to for the rest of your life. Marriage will change you both; that is why seeking counseling prior to and after getting married is the healthiest option for couples to remain in a healthy marriage.

Regular Question Sessions

Taking time out to communicate with each other is a major key factor. When you communicate it keeps the relationship on the same page. So remain transparent and set aside time to talk with no distractions coming in between your growth.

Still Date

While in the honeymoon phase of marriage couples tend to spend more time together and as time goes on romance begins to fade. However, couples should take time out to go on dates even if this is once a month it should be often enough to keep you both reminded why you both fell in love. After having kids, working constantly, and having busy schedules there has to be time to have a date night. Dating while married keeps the relationship fresh and ever growing.

Wherever you are in your love journey be sure to trust in God. Have faith and remain steadfast. If you fall dust yourself off and get back up. We as Black women have been through so many heartbreaks, still never let those relationship disasters deter your destiny. Great things are soon to come. Single ladies who might be dating know your worth and never settle, hold high standards and keep bettering yourself while God prepares the man of your dreams, the one you deserve. Married women stay true to love and respect and cherish the love God blessed you with.

Love is patient, love is kind. It does not envy, it does not boast, it is not proud. It is not rude, it is not self-seeking, it is not easily angered, it keeps no record of wrongs. Love does not delight in evil but rejoices with the truth.

1 Corinthians 13;1

Changed by Love

by Brittani N. Roberson

As a young child, I remember watching my parents and thinking "What's the point of being in a relationship?" I developed the idea that love was painful very early on in life. I would sit in my room and crawl under my covers waiting for the screaming and fighting to stop. With my heart pounding and tears flowing, my mind would race at the thought that these were two people who said they loved each other. It was so confusing to me. How do two people who love each other so much not care about hurting each other so much? And the question I asked myself even more was "Why would someone choose to be in a relationship if this is how it is?" What I did not know at the time was that all relationships did not look unhealthy like this. How

85

could I know? Both sets of my grandparents had been divorced and remarried and eventually my parents would find themselves divorced also. Were they just following in their parents' footsteps? If that's the case, how could I ever have any chance of having a happy successful relationship? Well, if you asked me this a little over a decade ago, I would have said my chances are pretty slim. But for those who know me, most likely you are aware that I am in a beautifully healthy relationship. Please understand that getting to this wonderful love I found was not an overnight love story. There were many relationships and "situationships" I had to go through before I reached the gold at the end of the rainbow.

So, I talked about the beauty at the end of the rainbow, but what was at the beginning of the rainbow? Well, let me tell you! There were arguments, disrespect, jealousy, insecurities and a whole lot of other negative characteristics that I am not proud of. You could not tell me that I wasn't with "the one". We were what I used to call a perfect match. We argued with each other like no other couple I knew. I knew that when a man takes the time to argue with you, that it means he is passionate and devoted to the relationship. The second way I just knew I was with the love of my life was because we were both jealous and insecure. Again, I just knew that if he didn't want me around any guys but him, it just meant he loved me and wanted all of my attention. I could go on and on about the many ways I knew we were a match made in heaven, but we would be here for days, maybe even months. Well, I hope by now you are picking up on my sarcastic tone, because lord knows that we were terrible for each other. As foolish as my justification for an unhealthy relationship may seem, this was really the thought process that I had at that time. Unfortunately, a lot of young women have this same mindset. We trick ourselves in believing that a person's jealousy and overbearing personalities are gestures of caring. When in reality, it only means that they do not respect you.

FAITHFULNESS & RELATIONSHIPS

So, earlier on I gave you a hint that at some point in my relationship journey there was a change for the better. But, before I get to my new relationship, let's discuss how the old toxic relationship ended. It was the middle of my freshman year in college. After five long years, my ex told me that he was done with me. The only explanation was that he didn't want to hurt me anymore, nothing more nothing less. What is the strongest synonym for the word pain that comes to your mind? Whatever you came up with, that's what I felt. I was devastated. I felt like I was unworthy and not good enough for anyone else. I wanted to drop out of school. I lay in bed for a few days wondering how I would ever get over this pain. What I didn't realize at that time was that I was more in love with the idea of "us". I was more worried about the years we put in, even though a majority of that time was miserable. Because I had this false idea of what love was, I put myself through more heartache and pain than I needed to. When we go through our first heartbreak, we often feel like we will never bounce back. Every situation, relationship, and story are all a part of a bigger picture and a lesson learned. I thought I would never make it through that pain. Not only did I make it through, but I found a love much healthier and stronger. More importantly, the lessons that I learned about myself helped me to handle my next relationship. Well maybe not in the beginning, but at some point, I began to let go of those negative characteristics that were ruining my relationship and learn healthier more positive ways of dealing with people in general.

So, now what? That's the question I asked myself over and over, until one day, I met this guy that I like to call Shug. He was cute, but I wasn't rushing anything after what I had just been through. I won't lie; in order to make myself feel better I was tempted to jump right in. Shug and I spent almost every day of that summer together. We hung out and laughed like little kids. We would stay up all times of the night learning about each other. I had never experienced anything like it. The more I chilled with him, the more I started to feel like I liked him. He started to express his feelings for me. But! He had an infant son! You know people had a whole lot to say about that. "You don't want no baby mama drama", "you're too young to be a stepmom", and on and on. Although some of the things they said were true I needed to make my own decision, and that decision was not to make anyone make me feel forced to make a decision.

I was going to do what was best for me and that was exactly what I did. I remained friends with Shug for about eight months before I decided to commit to a relationship with him. This was the best decision I could have ever made for myself and for my relationship. It gave me time to heal and also allowed us to build a strong bond and mutual affection that comes with being someone's friend. We too often rush into another situation because it makes us feel better in the moment, but a temporary fix will only cause more heartache and pain down the road. *Outside of your relationship with God, the most important relationship you can pour into is your relationship with yourself.*

Once Shug and I finally decided to be in a committed relationship, everything was not all sugar and roses. Remember the beginning of that rainbow we talked about? Well, those same insecurities and negative characteristics had not yet been unlearned. I had grown so used to thinking that the way a man showed you he loved is by being controlling, that I actually believed that Shug did not love and care about me because he was not questioning me about where I was going or who I was with. I recall calling him and telling him that I was going out to the club with my girlfriends. I was waiting for him to begin grilling me. I waited. And I waited some more, and I waited some more. His exact words were "ok be careful and call me when you get home". I was flabbergasted, and even more than that I was pissed off. I said, "So what you don't care about me"? That day he made it very clear that we were both adults and that if we could not trust each other enough to be able to go places without each other then we should not be together. Well, he told me.

FAITHFULNESS & RELATIONSHIPS

You would think that I would have been happy right? Well, I wasn't. I was hurt. This was such a backwards thought process. My negative cognitions would continue to creep in and trick me into believing false messages. So how did I change you ask? It started by changing my negative thought processes. When you change the way you think about something, it changes the way you feel, which then changes the way you react. It's a chain effect. So let me give you an example. One thing that used to really grind my gears was when my husband didn't ask me if I wanted some of his food. Even though it wasn't a huge deal, it still really agitated me. If I asked him for a bite, he would always share, and half the time I didn't even want any of his food but in my mind, it was the principal. So often, in my past allowed "the principal" has made a situation worse than it really needed to be. I digress, back to changing negative thoughts. So, I changed my thought process from "It is so rude that he doesn't want to share with me" to "It's nice that anytime I ask him to share with me whether he wants to or not".

See, we try to force people to feel and think the way we want them to. Why did it matter if he wanted to give it to me or not as long as he gave it to me? Once I changed that thought process it changed the way I felt. I went from feeling angry and agitated to feeling grateful. This obviously changed the way I reacted. Instead of walking around with an attitude all day I would show him I appreciated him sharing with me, which in turn made him feel better for sharing with me and made him want to share with me more. I know this is a small example, but often it's the small things that drive a wedge in the relationship. The more I applied the concept of changing negative thoughts and distortions, the easier problem solving became.

While working on changing myself, I also started paying attention to other couples that were successful and appeared happy. My mom was now in a happy healthy relationship and so was my grandmother. I started pulling from their relationships what I thought would make us stronger. With ups and downs we continued to build. Then finally we made it official. You would have thought with one honorary child and two other kids that we would have already been official. But nope, we did not get married before we had children. Speaking of children, let me explain to you how children affected our relationship. We have five beautiful children, three boys and two girls. Their ages are 12, 9, 6, 2, and 2. Yup, I have twins. As beautiful as my babies are, they definitely have tested our relationship. We have dealt with baby mama drama, custody battles, and differences of opinions on raising children.

The most difficult thing we experienced in regard to our children was the fact that four of our children were born premature. My first-born child particularly almost broke us. He was born at 24 weeks, weighing one pound 8 oz. The doctors told us that my baby wouldn't make it and that if he did, he would be significantly disabled. He was in the hospital for about 6 months. At the time I was in graduate school finishing up my master's degree in social work. This level of stress was new for both of us. We had never experienced anything of this caliber. As we both tried to grapple with reality that we may lose our son, we began to grow apart. We both had so much displaced anger and we began taking it out on each other. We were both grieving in two completely different ways. My way to cope was to go to school during the day and spend the rest of the night at the hospital. His way of coping was to write music, be in the studio, and chill with his boys. This infuriated me. I thought because he didn't grieve like me that it meant he did not care about our son. This negative thought process made me feel very angry which made me lash out at him. I thought we were over. But as things began to turn around for our son our tolerance for each other began to grow. All it took was one real raw conversation. It was not comfortable, but it was necessary. Through that conversation we learned so much about each other. We vowed from that day forward we always have those conversations, even when they are difficult. The reality in any relationship is that difficult times will come. It's all about learning from those difficult times so you know how to handle them moving forward.

During our next rough patch, we were ready to rock and roll. We had three children and had just gotten married. Life was great. Of course, things can't stay good for too long before the devil will try to throw you off. We returned from our honeymoon and I was ready to get back to work. I was a program supervisor for a nonprofit social service agency. I had so many plans I was ready to embark on. Then boom! I found I was pregnant. Not only was I pregnant, but I was pregnant with twins. When I tell you I almost passed out when I heard the word twins. How do we go from three to five children? Well, the bombshells kept coming. I became very ill and had to go on bed rest, I lost my grandfather, and I ended up having the twins at 29 weeks. They weighed 2lbs. Here we go again. Not only did they end up staying in the hospital, but I developed two pulmonary embolisms (blood clots) in my lungs that almost killed me. I was admitted to the same hospital as the twins. Meanwhile Shug was trying to hold the fort down. The stress was becoming so overwhelming for him that it began manifesting itself in his health. Guess who else ended up in the hospital. Yup, you guessed it. Shug was admitted to the hospital to deal with some bad gastrointestinal issues he was experiencing. As stressful as this situation was, we knew that we were in it together. This time around we were genuinely concerned about the other person. Together we made it through.

There were plenty of other difficult situations that came our way. Just to name a few: finances, balancing healthy relationships with children, balancing work, maintaining intimacy, different viewpoints, role reversal, different education levels, blended family, loss of family members, health problems and so much more. To be able to support someone through traumas like these is a *next level love*. Only a real friend will ride with you through it all. Shug and I allowed these situations to bring us closer together. At this point we are inseparable.

91

As I write about my journey through this thing we call love, I can't help but to feel so amazingly blessed. Twelve years ago, we were a young couple with no idea what direction we were coming or going, to what some believe to be a power couple. I am a licensed social worker and Shug has a successful street wear brand. In order to be a power couple, you have to invest just as much into your partner as you do yourself. That's not always easy, but it is necessary. Shug took on the stay-at-home parent role so that I could focus on school and my career during the time he was having health issues. I reciprocated this by giving him hundred percent of my support for him to dive completely into being a business owner. Despite the judgment we got from other people about our role reversals and our nontraditional path, we committed to staying loyal to each other. To sum it up, some other important changes we made to improve our love story were; changing thought process and unrealistic expectations, accepting each other for who we really are, caring about your partner's happiness as much as you care about your own, not communicating/arguing to prove your point, learning to listen to what he/she is actually saying vs. what you "think" they mean, validating each other's feelings, accepting what your partner "feels" even when it wasn't your intentions to make them feel that way and acknowledging those feelings, supporting each other's dreams and learning each other's love language. When you make these changes, you can have it all.

Sharing the hardships of my relationship has not been an easy process. However, I want couples, especially young Black couples, to understand that love is not about a butterfly feeling. It's about supporting each other and being loyal to each other even when things don't "feel" good. Loving someone is a choice. Having a healthy relationship is a choice, and that is what makes love beautiful. Some would say the odds were against us. But it wasn't for them to decide what was for us.

Love and faith go hand and hand. You have to have faith to acquire true love.

"Love is patient, love is kind. It does not envy, it does not boast, it is not proud. It does not dishonor others, it is not self-seeking, it is not easily angered, it keeps no record of wrongs. Love does not delight in evil but rejoices with the truth. It always protects, always trusts, always hopes, always perseveres."

1 Corinthians 13: 4-7

END

Worthy

by Lois McFadden

I was blessed to be raised in a small town in New Jersey with both my mother and father in the house. Before I was exposed to Family Matters, The Cosby's and other sitcoms with various family dynamics, they were my first example of what family and love looked like. They were not perfect because perfect doesn't exist, but they were together, and as far as I can remember, they were happy. As with any relationship, I'm sure they had their ups and downs, but with communication and respect, they pushed through and set a positive example of true unconditional love. In my mind, this was the norm, but life has a way of proving us wrong.

I have always been a lover of love; it is so complex yet simply beautiful. Nevertheless, I was never one to sit and dream of the day *I* got married or plan the whole experience out, Honestly, I was never on a mission to "find love". I figured it would come to me in God's time. Of course, I had experiences of young love, but that understandably dwindled away as I grew older and entered the real world. In my early 20s, I met a young man whom I instantly clicked with. We had common interests and started off as just friends. The friendship soon formed into something more, and we became official. The weeks turned to months, the months into years. Along the way I saw so many wonderful qualities in this man and so much potential in the things that he could accomplish. But I also saw a lot of characteristics that I did not favor, and that slowly began to tear me down emotionally, but love is blind, and I continued to see the potential in him. Although we created countless memories that will forever hold a place in my heart, in my mind, I knew something wasn't right. I knew that the way we communicated wasn't right. I knew that the level of respect presented to me was subpar. I knew that I deserved better. But I wanted this because I love him, right? Wrong! My insecurities were leading the way; "Could I find a better mate?" "Am I enough?" "Starting over is going to take forever." "My parents never quit on love." "What am I doing wrong?" All were valid concerns and questions, but I was on the inside looking out; my vision was clouded. So, I stayed. Through the pain I prayed for patience, guidance and understanding. I always thought if I gave 110% it would all fall into place. Soon I learned that no matter how much you may want something it may not be meant for you and God will show you one way or another.

Shortly after the birth of our child, we decided that the relationship had run its course, and although it's not what I wanted, I know it's what God wanted for me.

I knew it's what I needed. It wasn't easy; some nights I silently cried myself to sleep. Other nights, sleep never found me because my mind was too busy racing. Should I run back to him like I had done so many times in the past? How is co-parenting going to work? I would find myself holding my sleeping six-month-old baby boy saying, "I'm sorry I never wanted it to be like this." "This is not the life I had growing up." "This is not the plan I had for you." I can sit here and say proudly that I am glad God is the author and the master of all things because He knew, and my story was already written.

I took time after the relationship to reflect on how our love story started, grew and eventually ended. Along the path, I realized that I didn't stand up for myself or set boundaries, I became submissive and silenced. This allowed room for disrespect and belittlement. I opened the door for this behavior, yet I felt resentment when it continued. As I reflected on the situation as a whole, I had to take responsibility for my role in the relationship and how it affected the outcome.

I was so concerned with trying to please him that I forgot about myself along the way. I had to take time to find happiness in myself again. I felt every emotion, anger, joy, fear and everything in between. The journey wasn't easy; luckily, I was blessed with supportive friends and family. Although I rarely let them see the pain that I felt, they comforted me with their presence and their undying love. As the days went on, I felt a little more like me, my smile felt brighter and my laugh more genuine. I was able to heal in my time, on my terms. I focused on the blessings and lessons instead of the hurt. I was able to enjoy all the wonderful moments and the indescribable love that comes along with being a mother. I thank God every day for choosing me to be his mom and blessing him with a father who wants to be in his life regardless of our past. I prayed daily for patience and love to raise him as I blindly traveled down an unfamiliar path of parenthood.

I had been on a journey of self-love and acceptance so long that I became comfortable in my single lifestyle. Although years had passed and I was open to love again, I was in no rush. I prayed for God to mold me and send me what is meant for me in His time. His time came sooner than expected, what seemed to be, out of nowhere came a fresh breath of air. He was charming, patient, an effective communicator and most importantly God fearing. So many attributes I value in a man, yet I was not easily persuaded. He was understanding of my hesitance while being confidently persistent in his pursuit to be a part of my world. I knew this was God at work. Whether it be for a season or a lifetime it was a necessary part of the process for me to see that I am worthy. I am worthy of a man who is appreciative of the woman I am, a man who reminds me of the light I possess in my darkest of times and tells me I am beautiful just in case I forgot. I am worthy of a man who gives Godly counsel and walks in faith. I am worthy of love.

We as women are natural nurturers, often giving our all to those who are not deserving. We must always remember to love ourselves and know that we are worthy. It is vital to set boundaries, speak up and require respect. Acknowledge and learn from your mistakes so you can move forward. Be humble and patient until God provides what is for you. Pray in the hardest of times and praise in your most joyous moments. To every woman who has read these words, know that you are WORTHY! 4 Love is patient, love is kind. It does not envy, it does not boast, it is not proud. 5 It does not dishonor others, it is not self-seeking, it is not easily angered, it keeps no record of wrongs. 6 Love does not delight in evil but rejoices with the truth. 7 It always protects, always trusts, always hopes, always perseveres.

8 Love never fails. But where there are prophecies, they will cease; where there are tongues, they will be stilled; where there is knowledge, it will pass away. 9 For we know in part and we prophesy in part, 10 but when completeness comes, what is in part disappears. 11 When I was a child, I talked like a child, I thought like a child, I

reasoned like a child. When I became a man, I put the ways of childhood behind me. **12** Now we see only a reflection as in a mirror; then we shall see face to face. Now I know in part; then I shall know fully, even as I am fully known.

13 And now these three remain: faith, hope and love. But the greatest of these is love.

1 Cor 13:4-13

END

God Still Loves Me

by Camilah Thierry

If my mom had not been snooping through my phone in December of 2014, I suppose my life would still be the same. I would probably still be putting on a façade in front of family and friends and trying my hardest to avoid any conversation about the "L" word. But my life changed drastically when my mom uncovered a truth that I had tried my hardest to bury, that I was sexually attracted to women. Seventeen-year-old me would say this was the worst (thing) that could have happened. I had heard all my life how the pastor condemned gay people in church, and I did not want to be a member of a group that God could not love. However, life has a weird way of working itself out because I ended the year of 2014 feeling like the spokesperson of this group in my house. During the beginning of this journey everything seemed so unsure. A lot of questions ran through my mind nonstop. "Does God love?", "Will I ever heal and learn to love myself?", and "Would I ever experience a true and real love?" Twenty-three-year-old me now knows the answer to all of these questions is a strong YES. December of 2014 significantly changed my life in two ways; I began my own close and intimate walk with Christ, and I learned how to genuinely love myself and others.

The most heart wrenching question I battled with was "Does God still love me?" All church people who were so high and mighty and had never sinned before (or so it would appear) would answer no. According to this group, what I was facing had eternally condemned me to hell and God had definitely turned His back on me. This was a hard reality for a seven-teen-year old to face, but I did what I thought was best at the time and completely quit going to church. If God could not love me and neither could the people who claimed to be serving Him, then I would not love them either. But my inner man, specifically my spirit man who is who I really am, would not let me rest on this. I struggled to find peace. I tried to find it in people, but my relationships would always fail; fast. So, one day I cried out to God exposing all the hurt that I hid from feeling condemned by the world. He answered me saying, "Get to know me for yourself." You see, I had been listening to people this whole time, people who are stuck in their OWN worldly ways, so I needed to go to the source myself. I started this journey by reading the Gospels: Matthew, Mark, Luke, and John. I wanted to get to know my Lord and Savior who laid down His life for me on a more intimate level.

Through reading the Gospels I quickly learned that I was loved by Christ, and that when He said "Lo, I am with you always even until the end of the world" (Matthew 28:20) He was talking to me too! I held on tightly to this beautiful and rewarding promise. It was the reason I kept on reading and going before God trying to understand exactly what He thought about me. The second scripture I still hold onto can be found in Romans 8 verse 1. "Therefore, there is now no condemnation for those who are in Christ Jesus." Here it is stated why the gospel is such great news for those who believe. There was no room for condemnation for those of us who are in Christ Jesus. I learned that if I placed all of my hope and faith in Christ I was not condemned. So, all those pastors and church people were wrong. I did not have to walk around feeling defeated, no; I learned that victory through Christ Jesus was just as much mine as anyone else who calls on His name!

Becoming closer to God helped me learn to truly love myself, and it made me more confident to stop hiding what I was GROWING through. For a while, I focused all of my attention on standing on my own with Christ, and it was when I stopped looking for love that it found me. I will always remember the day this beautiful woman walked, well strutted, into my life. Not just beautiful physically, but her inner beauty is truly paramount. I know most parents teach their children that you cannot find love until you learn to love yourself, but I believe there are radiant people in the world that can help you on that journey. That is what she is for me. She introduced me to a genuine love that I honestly never thought I would experience. She did this by first loving me out loud and boldly. As soon as we started dating seriously, I was not her "secret lover". She did not hide me from her parents but confidently introduced me as the woman she was dating. And in the age of a strong social media presence, she still did not pretend I was just her little friend. All 3,000+ of her followers on Instagram found out quickly that I was her girlfriend, and when anyone had an issue with her decision to date me, she would quickly tell them to unfollow her. She has never tolerated any type of homophobia from friends or family. Her ability to check someone for our love was strikingly unmatched and quickly boosted my self-esteem.

For the first time in my life, I was not in a closet relationship and it is hard to describe accurately how really freeing this was for me. She absolutely surpassed any expectation I had for our relationship. Pursuing a relationship with her was life-altering. We helped each other grow in ways I am sure we both could write a book about. But I believe most importantly our love taught me how to be completely vulnerable with someone and love them beyond my own selfish desires.

My journey has only just begun, but I have learned that what I went through at seven-teen was just growing pains. When life seemed to be beating me down, it was actually preparing me for a stronger and more intimate walk with Christ. My Heavenly Father undoubtedly loves me and wants to see me happy. He's holding my hand every step of the way on this journey, and He has not forsaken me!

END

3

Health & Self-Care

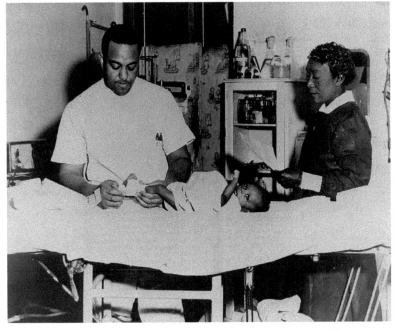

Doctor and nurse provide health care in the black community (circa 1960s)

MIND

What happens to the Black women's mental health? Does it come second or third because her life consists of pouring into everyone else, so she neglects her mental health? Mental health in the Black community is a "hush hush" conversation that usually is laughed off and pushed to the backburner. The stigma of mental health in the Black community is pervasive because most know no better. It is instilled within the Black community that mental health conditions are a sign of weakness. Most just seek out help from their faith bases; for the majority, that place is church. Data shows that within the Black community, Black women's symptoms of mental illnesses are intensified when compared to their White counterparts.

ANXIETY

To truly understand why Black women are the way they are, you must first understand how Black women are viewed in this society. The reputation of the Black Woman is independent, angry, and aggressive, all of which play symbolic roles in the topic of mental health. These stereotypes that our country has plastered all over have a way of unconsciously contributing to our anxiety levels. The Black Woman who will lash out and curse out someone without thinking twice is what's often portrayed. This has a way of conditioning Black Women into following these rollercoaster behaviors.

SOCIAL ANXIETY

Unaware, oftentimes a Black Woman is the only one in the workplace, *"Walking into any room, usually as the only Black woman, I knew that I had this superpower of being able to feel both invisible and hyper-visible at the same time." (Kendiel, 2020)* Could you imagine going to work, school, or even stores and not having anyone there who looks like you? By having someone that you can relate to allows the defense wall to come down. We seem to be the only race that accepts everyone else, but it's seldom mutual.

PTSD

Post-Traumatic Stress Disorder (PTSD) is the highest among Black women, studies have proven. Being a Black woman in America comes with trauma at some point in your life, no matter who you are. The trauma in one's life impacts someone's life even when they might say it didn't, given the prevalence of trauma Black women have shown a wide range of major traumatic cases, *"The rate of sexual assault among Black women is 3.5 times higher than that of any other group in this country. Black women are also less likely to report their assault. Many suffer in silence for years, never sharing with anyone what has happened to them. Thus, the trauma remains unnamed, unknown and untreated and the symptoms worsen."* (Angela Neal-Barnett, PhD, 2018) Your surroundings have a way of drawing from you, and in the community, Black women live in the majority. So, the emotions that are most felt are hopelessness and sadness. Depression, stress, and anger all work together during PTSD, and trailing all of these is Substance use Disorder (SUD).

SUD

Substance use Disorder is prevalent among Black women because of all the things that are lacking in as resources. Due to the lack of education and resources to assist with rehabilitation, most Black women who suffer with this illness never fully receive the help they could benefit from. It's common to find more liquor stores in a predominantly Black community than health resources. Data revealed, *"6.9% of African Americans have a substance use disorder compared to a rate of 7.4% among the total population."* (Kaliszewski, 2020) These low-income areas are infested with drugs and substance abuse. Oftentimes, Black women choose to cope by self-medicating. In the United States, African American communities show significant dissimilarity when compared to other races.

DEPRESSION

DOES DEPRESSION IMPACT BLACK WOMEN? Depression is one of the numerous mental illnesses that need to be confronted head on, especially within the Black community. According to *Black Women's Imperative, nearly* 10% of Black women say they feel *"everything's an effort."* Let's make one thing clear: Depression is not feeling sad one day or having the blues for a week. The following are all red flags for depression: Anxiety, sadness, irritability, guiltiness, restlessness, hopelessness are all signs to go get help. Black women tend to ignore the signs in most cases and attempt to patch their pain with *"emotion fillers"*. *Emotion fillers* are just forms of quick fixes. Very often these *"emotion fillers"* wind up being food, alcohol, or drugs. Depression is a slow silent internal killer. Depression has no economic preference or age preference. Compared to any other race, Black women are the highest risk for depression. This may be partially due to what the Black woman has to endure each and every day. The struggles and hurdles of being a Black woman can be exhausting, overwhelming and lonely. Therapy or medication are the two most common ways of treating depression.

"I had no job prospects; I could not afford the classes and I was borderline DEPRESSED!" (Williams, 2020)

Growing Pains
I'm sorry depression we've been friends long enough
Addiction we've been friends long enough
Anxiety you got to go now your time is up
Hot temper I'm leaving you out in the cold to freeze
JEALOUSY!
Go back to wherever you came from

FEAR!

Exit my mind body and spirit

There's no room for you in my life anymore

I refuse to ignore the growing pains any longer

Conniving parasite "so called" friends

Suicidal thoughts you are blocked forever

Fake friends call

Let it go straight to voicemail

Lies and rumors you lose this fight

Me finding me

Unlocked the chains of depression

That open the door of new beginnings

Poem By: Jasmine Poole

DOES DEPRESSION IMPACT BLACK WOMAN?

I FEEL	BLACK WOMAN	WHITE WOMAN
SAD	3.9%	2.9%
HOPELESS	2.4%	1.9%
WORTHLESS	1.8%	1.6%

MENTAL HEALTH & WELLNESS TIPS

- **Research Family Health History**
- **Journal Your Mood Changes**
- **Create Healthy Boundaries**
- **Take Time Out for Fun & Relaxing Activities**
- **Join Support Groups**
- **Normalize Therapy**
- **Make Yourself A Priority**
- **It Is Okay to Ask for Help**
- **Prayer**
- **Time to Process Emotions**

A Love That Heals

Shenee L. Omuso, MAT, MA, CCC-SLP

In this season of my life, I dwell in a new place. An unfamiliar place. A place that excites. A place of confidence and self-acceptance. A place of optimism and hope. A place of celebration and life. I am so consumed with this place, desiring to be wrapped in its warmth and fullness because I can remember when life in my twenties was so different. It wasn't until I was in my thirties that at the core of my being, in that still small place that speaks if you listen, I had a revelation. The deep, overwhelming sense of sadness, anger and frustration whose weight I had become used to carrying was rooted in this truth: I had never experienced what it means to love myself, and I didn't know how to. Most people do not walk around and shout that they hate themselves, but it is evident that my choices, the behavior I demonstrated towards myself, and the years of negative self-talk could only mean one thing – I did not love the person I was and that the grace I so willingly gave to others, I did not extend to myself. As a result of my self-hatred and rejection, my warped idea of love was found in other people and that the measure of love they gave was based on my perfection and performance instead of the truth that I am worth loving, first by me and then by others.

My quest for perfection started well before adulthood, in fact, it began at an incredibly young age. Growing up in a Christian home, I mistakenly understood God's love (and wrath) to be directly tied to my ability to obey the teachings of the Bible. If I didn't obey, I feared the consequences. I feared that I would be punished, and if I kept messing up, I would be punished even more. This was because I didn't believe I deserved forgiveness, patience or kindness. So, I decided very early on that I had to be perfect to avoid God's wrath. This translated to my relationship with my parents. I knew they loved me, but I figured they would love me more if I performed well. I became consumed with accomplishment. I was known for my bright smile and friendly personality, good grades and of course my long Black hair with not a strand out of place. I continued my path of being an overachiever through high school, college, grad school, and my second masters, graduating every program Summa Cum Laude. By the time I was twenty-five, I had traveled to over seven countries, serving in orphanages, training hundreds of young people in leadership and performing arts, rebuilding homes in Haiti, researching unknown languages and cultures in South America and bringing medicine and health education to small villages in Africa. But the cost of being loved by so many and not myself first slowly started to add up.

My breaking point came at the age of twenty-six. I remember the sheer exhaustion I felt from trying to be everything to everyone, but I was nothing to myself. Approval, acceptance, love, approval, acceptance, love. Approval, acceptance, love. That was the record on repeat, and I didn't care what I had to do to hear that song play. So, I compromised my morals and conceded any power that I had until I was diagnosed with a rare condition called Trigeminal Neuralgia, a neurological disorder of the face known for riddling its host with the worst pain outside of childbirth. This condition had to have been brought on by severe stress and mental turmoil because tests revealed there were no physical causes. Rather, it was like I could physically feel my mind and heart snap and my body paid for it. I remember describing myself as an open nerve, every action and interaction was magnified, my emotions so sensitive to the touch. I could feel the tears bubbling behind the mask, ready to flood out at any moment. I remember climbing the walls in pain and the drugs that kept me in a numbed state of reality. I remember feeling as if I was on the outside watching my life being lived and despite the good I was doing, I was not happy, not fulfilled because I was doing it with the wrong intention in my heart. I had evolved into a "human doing" vs. a "human being", killing myself every day because I had wrongfully learned that performance and perfection was my barometer for love and worth, and from here it would only become more severe.

Two years later, after graduating with my second masters I woke up one morning to a small test on my nightstand that revealed I was not only pregnant but unmarried and jobless. I stood there, not excited, not thrilled for the possibility of life growing inside of me. No, the first thing I felt was shame. Not Shenee the youth pastor and young women's leader. Not Shenee the smart, ambitious, Christian woman whose life and career were just starting. I was more devastated by what others would think of me than happy for the gift of motherhood. I was the biggest fraud in history, or so I thought. Pregnant! I could taste the fruit of bitterness, anger, rage, torment, sadness, insecurity and fear daily. I had become one with the pain of disappointment, shame, regret, self-condemnation and low self-esteem I experienced day in and day out. I secretly felt defined by it. Who was I without it? To pursue freedom was much scarier than staying a slave to discouragement, depression and unforgiveness. So, I chose the type of suffering that did not make me better, that did not liberate or that I could learn from. No, I chose the type of suffering that kept me a victim, kept me paralyzed and feeling unworthy.

After wrestling for nine months with all these overwhelming thoughts and emotions, my daughter was born. Her birth prompted a new journey. I became committed to evolving into the woman I could see in my mind and feel in my heart. I realized that the woman I was and the woman I wanted to become were not two different, distant beings. No, I was that woman, I needed to rid myself of some terrible, errant ways of thinking and embrace some new behaviors. I was full of so many personal and professional aspirations, but I knew I did not want to get where I wanted to be and not like the person I was when I got there. So, I had to do (and still have to do) some work.

The liberation I feel to love and accept every part of me has been accomplished by applying four of self-love I discovered through a whole lot of prayer, classes, journaling, mediation and conversation.

1. I am strongest when I allow myself to be humble. Humility is a constant state of being that allows me to be molded into a more conscious, aware, accountable and grateful person. Living so long basking in my accomplishments and being defined by them caused pride and judgment to take root. Pride says I have the RIGHT to have my way, to be heard, to not be wronged. Pride boasts that you are the problem and not me. Pride is always ready to defend and is easily offended. It causes you to not deal with or hide the ugly truths of who you are or blames others for that ugliness. But authentically loving me has shown me I have

nothing to hide, prove or defend. Living in humility means living in a place that seeks reconciliation, connection and space for open mindedness and change.

2. I must embrace the beauty of each season no matter how barren or abundant it may seem because I am worthy of good things. I had to grieve those dreams I held in my heart as a little girl. The choices I made did not lead me down the aisle wearing a White wedding dress and living in a house with a two-car garage. No, my lack of self-love leads to hardship and to dreams deferred. That meant I had to refocus and redefine myself by new dreams because holding on to the old ones were hindering me from experiencing the fullness of who I was becoming and the endless possibilities of what my life could be. I learned to live without the anxiety of planning and knowing every detail of my life, how to release regret and loss, how to not be consumed with finding my purpose and being jealous or comparing myself with others. Rather, I began to understand that days make up seasons and seasons make up our lives. Now, who I dedicate myself to becoming each day is important. How much energy I give people and situations matters. Having a healthy, balanced perspective about who and where I am in life is a priority and a reason to push forward.

3. My mental and emotional stability is a choice I make moment to moment. I was guilty of what can be termed "double mindedness". This is the pattern of thinking that believes one thing one moment, but this thought easily changes, easily doubts, easily retreats and is easily influenced. One moment I am strong and capable and the next moment I can never do anything right. One moment I am full of faith about an issue and the next and I am full of doubt that it will happen. This daily roller coaster of emotion was exhausting and unproductive. Now, I have learned to make a conscious choice every moment to stand on fact instead of feeling. The fact is I am everything God created me to be and more. The fact is my identity is not wrapped up in what I do or don't do. The fact is

every day I make mistakes, I fail, and I come up short. The fact is I am better, I do better, and I want better every day. My challenge is to declare these things over my life in the moments when I want to give up, when I speak negatively about myself, when the situation seemingly warrants fear instead of faith.

4. Perfection is lethal to my development as a woman, wife and mother. I have wrestled in secret with pain I have experienced in my life for as long as I can remember. I did not believe I could share my authentic me and still be understood, loved or respected by others. Who wants to look like, much rather admit, their life is falling apart? Instead, I suffered in silence and drowned in isolation because of the image I felt I needed to maintain. I loved the love and admiration I received for so many reasons. I loved appearing to work hard and accomplish great things because then at least I had something. The problem came when those things were not enough. When the pieces of my life became exposed to others and I could no longer hold it together. Understand this; the prison of perfection is a different type of prison in that the door is always open. There is no lock on the door. I made a choice to stay there instead of walking out. Every time I would get the courage to take one step out, I would again be pushed back by people's perception of me and the need for acceptance. So, I stayed there crying out, "Does anyone see me, does anyone love me for me?" But soon I saw me and for the first time, I loved me.

So, I will continue to dwell and thrive in this place devoid of performance and perfectionism, a place devoid of shame and defeat, loss and rejection. I look at my husband and beautiful children and I am thrilled that I can finally receive and give them the love they deserve because I understand what it means to love myself. My never-ending journey to love myself means to keep the promises I make to myself, to trust myself when doubt creeps in, to spend time embracing how beautiful I am, to explore the secret passions of my heart and to make decisions out of pure intention and self-assurance. I am proud to speak from a place of growing clarity, wisdom and power because for so long I could not say that. I am proud that the work I do, I now do from a place of genuine love and honest compassion for others because what I do, I do not TO BE loved, but because I AM loved.

END

Hair salon in the mid 1900s

HAIR

"But for a woman, if her hair is abundant, it is a glory to her; for her hair is given to her for a covering." Corinthians 11:15 A Black woman's hair is her glory. You can be known for the picked-out afro like the Black activist Angela Davis, or the press and curl like Madam C.J. Walker the first Black woman to be a millionaire after starting her own hair care line, or the locks like the famous singer Lauryn Hill. From the beautiful brown sista with a head of silver-gray hair, "Gray hair is a crown of glory; it is gained in a righteous life." (Proverbs 16:3) To the little girl sitting between her mother's legs on the stoop as she gets her hair braided and beaded at the ends. The versatility is endless, from curly to straight or maybe braids or locks, "You can spend a lifetime discovering all the hairstyles, there are so many of them, and so many creative, natural styles yet to be invented." (Assata Shakur, 1987) We can't forget about the short or long weaves and wigs. Black women are often imitated but never duplicated. Our hair is a fashion statement many other races try to duplicate our beauty and style.

When talking about Black women and our hair, you can't forget the best part. The only place a Black woman truly goes to sit for eight to ten hours, other than church, is none other than the beauty salon, a pillar in the Black community. The beauty salon is a perfect example of how we support one another's businesses within our communities. The beauty salon is where women spend hours sharing advice, telling stories, and spreading other people's business. There's always a good laugh or therapeutic venting rant some woman goes on about her pain and current situation. The beauty salon is a Black woman's place to recharge from the world's draining stressors. It is a safe haven where Black queens take some time out for themselves.

When it comes to Black women and our hair, at night before bed, there is work to be done; you can pin it, curl it, roll it, twist it, swirl wrap it with bonnets, rags, scarves or even undergarments such as pantyhose to protect it. As time went on, Black women have learned about what protects and what damages our hair, like pressing our hair with the classic hot comb made of iron, which would burn your scalp and oftentimes your ears. Modern day knowledge has saved time and our hair. Time and research have shown us that the relaxers are made of chemicals, including lye and sodium hydroxide, which break and damage the hair follicles. So, after having spent decades frying, pressing, relaxing and damaging our natural hair, we have finally begun to take better care of our God given curl. Before becoming all natural there is a dreadful process called *"The Big Chop"*.

For many generations, we were taught to hate ourselves and want to straighten out natural hair and look as much like a White woman as possible, even if that means destroying our roots in the process, "I am hiding my beautiful, nappy hair under this wig and hating it, maybe we are all running and hiding. A whole generation of Black women hiding out under dead White people's hair. I pray and struggle for the day when we can all come out from under these wigs." (Assata Shakur, 1987) Every Black woman who ever had a relaxer and wanted to switch back over to natural hair understands what that takes. Being natural after having had the chemicals of a relaxer in your hair means that the *"The Big Chop"* awaits them.

Natural hair styles are making their way back into our culture again after being a thing of the past. Historically, 1960's and 1970's Black women modeled the afro-centric afro, all natural and beautifully healthy. Assata Shakur, a historic pro Black activist wrote about her experience with "The Big Chop" she said, "To make it natural, I literally had to cut the conk off." This process is very emotional because a Black woman's hair is how we express ourselves; this process definitely is a confidence builder and teaches the woman to love herself regardless of her hairstyle. After a few months of healthy treatment your hair begins to grow back and you start witnessing the growth right before your eyes, "At last my hair was free." (Assata Shakur, 1987) Black women constantly deal with implicit biases from the rest of humanity, "A classmate of mine, who happens to be a White male, walked by me and said, "Wow, Kendeil. I don't know how I'm going to be able to tell you apart from the other girl in our class." You know . . . the other girl with braids and glasses." At that moment, it was clear to me that he was referring to the only other Black woman in a lecture hall of 90 students." (Contributing Writer, Glover, 2020)

Doing hair

Royal Roots

My hair needs of nothing else

Tired of the sizzling hot comb on the stovetop

We refuse to continue being chemicalized

We are finished being tugged and pulled east and west

Parted in so many directions

Ripped, snipped, dyed and tangled into bondage

Covered by wigs, weaves and clip-ons

My face is tired

ENOUGH

With the cosmetics

Contouring my nose to be slim

Or trying to shrink my lips

I AM ENOUGH NATURALLY

I am sick of being made over in a so-called makeover

Only a crown deserves to be kept on the roots of a queen

I am good, do not touch me

Poem By: Jasmine Poole

Nadia Bangura

Bang Dance Studio Instructor & Owner (2021)

BODY

CURVACEOUSNESS

Does the curvaceousness intimidate you? Or the sway of our hips and the thickness in our lips? Then why is it that so many still try to get surgery after surgery to look like us? The rest of the world constantly dismisses Black women's beauty in public, but behind closed doors every time you look, more and more people just finished getting silicone enhancements done to their bodies. Not all surgery is done with the intention of looking like a Black woman. However, the overall point is that oftentimes Black women are told they are not beautiful enough and that their bodies are too much. Your butt is too big! Your lips are oversized! Your thighs rub together! Your breasts are small or too large! No, your mirror is too small to reflect our beauty. Body shaming of the Black woman is a crime that is committed every day. If the world wants us to look different, they will have to take that up with God! Queens never apologize for being royalty. All women were wonderfully and beautifully sculpted by God.

You have the music video vixen that so many little Black girls watch on social media platforms, television and in movies, and from that image they construct what they think is beauty. Girls at an early age begin formulating video vixen descriptions in their minds. Again and again, this leads to disaster and self-esteem issues oftentimes. In all actuality, true beauty is what is within. So, queens ignore all self-doubt because it says in God's word the truth, *"I praise You, for I am fearfully and wonderfully made. Marvelous are Your works, and I know this very well."* *(Psalms 139:14)*

Although a queen's physical beauty is important, so is her inner health. The health conditions that disproportionately affect Black women the most: heart disease, stroke and diabetes, breast cancer, cervical cancer, fibroids, premature delivery, sickle cell disease, sexual transmitted disease, mental health issues. Black women suffer silently in the background terribly. Educating ourselves with these health issues will be the first step toward changing the stigma of the unhealthy Black woman. Records reveal the life expectancy for Black females is 76.1 years and 80 years for White females. Black women's health is a result of the life she has indoors and the lacking resources to health care. Throughout history, groups and organizations have formulated an attempt to provide healthcare to the Black community. A perfect example of this is, "The Panther Party had bought a brownstone on 127th Street, and as soon as it was renovated, we planned to open a free clinic there." (Assata Shakur. 1987) Despite this not lasting long in the 1970's, it was still a step in a positive direction to help strengthen the Black communities lacking healthcare resources. We as women, need to learn to simply embrace our curves no matter what race, size, or age you are. All women are beautiful. We should learn to embrace all bodies, no matter the jeans, or bra size.

Corinne Bradely-Powers (Owner)
Corinne's Place Soul Food Restaurant Est. 1989
(Camden NJ)

SOUL FOOD

Historically speaking African Americans heroically overcame centuries of oppression and throughout time brilliantly birthed "Soul Food". The deep-rooted delicious cuisine- fried chicken, deep fried catfish, smothered pork chops, pig's feet, baked mac-n-cheese, collard greens, Blacked-eyed-peas, candied yams- and red drink, along with something called "hard-times food", which is salt pork, or ham hocks, and cornbread. These have sustained generations of Black people during slavery, sharecropping, and much throughout history decades after. For many, these "Soul Food" dishes served as resourcefulness as well as culinary genius throughout the African American community. There are some critics who focus solely on the unhealthiness of this type of cooking. The progressive timeline of soul food will prove the influence and advances that have made it deserving of recognition and respect as the official African American cuisine.

In the early 1600's, slave owners controlled the amount of food that slaves received. More often than not, once a week slaves were dealt five pounds of starch (cornmeal, rice, and sweet potatoes), a few pounds of the cheapest scrap meats, and a jug of molasses. Needless to say, the enslaved African Americans supplemented their diet by fishing, hunting, and farming. The knowledge to raise livestock was passed down from West African culture. During this time slave masters ate out of the same pot but just different tables than the Black slaves. It was the touch of soul on every slave masters table that filled the bellies of generations of White families. Food is symbolic in the Black household because in the early 1800's, slaves would have one meal together as a family and the food was a way of fellowshipping with loved ones, *"A family of five usually gets about thirty pounds of fat side-pork and a couple of bushels of corn-meal a month."* *(WEB Du Bois, 1903)* Many critics use the term "slave food" naming it as unworthy to be categorized as an official cuisine.

After the ending of slavery and the start of sharecropping in the mid 1800's into the early 1900's, the development of the Black church strongly contributed to the birth of "soul food". Poor Blacks had to constantly borrow equipment needed to farm leaving them in debt and back at square one. The Civil War was yet an additional poverty pattern that constricted the dinner tables of African Americans during this time period. Black churches throughout history became known for their anniversary dinners, holiday events, and any other celebration in the Black community. These gatherings were most vital to the community during the time of sharecropping due to the debt acquired by Blacks on the plantations. Church functions served as a saving grace for so many struggling sharecropping Black families.

As time moved forward through the 1920's-1970, African Americans were on the move towards something safer, smarter, and greater (The Great

Migration). Many African Americans would call it "The Promised Land". Millions of African Americans relocated from the rural south to northern states like Philadelphia, New York, Maryland, and New Jersey. Around the concluding of World War II, the economic fortunes of African Americans brightened. This was an elevation time period for African Americans, new homes, more income to buy groceries. This growing prosperity enabled the birth of traditional Sunday dinners with a table of the special-occasion dishes.

At the beginning of the 1960's - 1990's, "Soul Food" was given its name. In the mid 1960's during the rise of "Black pride", many aspects of African American culture such as soul music were highlighted for their creative contribution and influence on American history. The term "Soul Food" was first used in 1964 at a peak moment in civil rights history for Black Americans. Soul food, in its most popular and recognizable form, comes to us thanks to "Soul Food" trailblazers like Camden restaurateur Corrine-Bradely-Powers, Sylvia Woods of Harlem and a multitude of home cooks. These fearless Southern cuisine entrepreneurs are the historians that keep the African American cuisine alive still today.

In today's society, food educators have found that Soul Food has taken healthier approaches. Many soul food restaurants today are more likely to use turkey instead of pork inside of side dishes like collard greens and green beans, which hold less sodium. These seemingly simple dietary staples in the historic soul food cuisine are extremely impactful. We see today that soul food has become the comfort food not just for African Americans whose ancestors invented it, but instead people of all races and cultures around the world.

At the Table

Welcome to the door to my taste buds

Crack open the front door to grandma's house

Mouthwatering deliciousness hits you within seconds

Skillet popping grease frying chicken and fish

Sending the fellas to grab a couple more bags of ice

Wrist turning patterns churning her famous potato salad

Fresh chopped carrots, onions, celery sprinkled spices

Diced chopped sliced steak resting on a bed of Jasmine rice

No measuring cups necessary

Pinches of grandmas love in every pot

Pots boiling on all four stove caps

Sizzling sounds of neck bones and collard greens joining together

As the food cooks, the family hounds and surrounds

Stories begin passed down from one generation to the next

Momma finishing up the baked mac and cheese

Simmering cheese grits melting down the sides of the pot

Memories are created as the house fills with delicious aromas

Mouths water, can't hardly wait to eat

Kids sneaking little samples as the tables being set

Grandma on the phone long distance with relatives down south

Imagine two sweet potato pies, strawberry and blueberry cheesecakes

Sitting on its throne at the end of the table is granny's famous five-layer red velvet

cake, sitting beside is the banana pudding everyone fights over

I hope you got a flavorful taste of what it's like at grandma's table

Grab a seat let's eat   Poem by Jasmine Poole

Weight Lifted

by Nita M.

Well, here we are sitting in the drive-thru at Hardee's on Valentine's Day Evening when we're asked, "How may I help you?" He looks at me and me at him, and I say, "You go first; I need more time." If I didn't weigh over 320 lbs., what would I or we be doing tonight? Would I be out dancing? Would I be on a romantic date night? I had hit the wall of frustration. I am done with living this way. So, it was back to me; it was my turn to order. What do I have tonight? One meal wouldn't make a difference, I thought. Then I thought back to the prior week's events. One of my favorite rap artists, Big Pun, had just passed away from a massive heart attack. He was a very overweight man, but young like me. I was 25 years old, a wife and a mother. I didn't want to leave my family at a young age too. So, I looked at my then husband and said, "I'll just have a diet soda." He looked puzzled and asked, "Are you sure?" I said, "Yup, Very."

126

The next morning, I woke up with the same level of determination in my heart. I was excited about this. When I lose this weight, I'm going to... If you've ever been on a weight loss journey, you know the future thoughts that help us get through the tough days. I made a picture hope journal and began to visualize the life I wanted to live. I would be able to shop for cute clothes, travel the world, and have a lover that admired and desired all of me!! I purchased a Richard Simmons weight loss program from an infomercial and began eating what I liked in moderation. And, for a while, it worked. I had also recently begun driving. I was well into my twenties before I started driving, because my then husband would make sure I got around. But my best friend at the time told me, "When you have a license to drive, you have freedom!" And that was something I longed for more than you even know; I wanted freedom. I then used my license to go to our local mall and walk laps. At first, I was too tired to make it more than halfway around the mall. But I kept going each day. I even signed my daughter up for gymnastics at one of the shops in the mall to help make sure I had a reason not to stay home.

Before long, I needed to step up my workouts, I began working out to the tougher workout videos. I joined Weight Watchers and learned about healthy food options based on their Points system. I began to eat more fruit and vegetables and drink more water. I also started to plan my meals around dinner. I knew if I ate well all day, I would have enough points to have a great dinner and possibly a healthy treat for dessert. Soon, people outside my home started to notice the changes in me physically as well as with my personality. I was happier, I had more energy, and most of all I had patience for the small issues that used to bother me. I was becoming whole, and within the span of a year and a half, I lost over 160 lbs. And although I was not finished with my weight loss journey, I was ready for my next goal which was finishing my undergraduate degree.

Finishing my degree was something I knew I had to do, not for anyone else except myself. But I also needed to do it to set an example for my daughter. I wanted my daughter to know that no matter what her past looked like, she could make her future look the way she envisioned. So, I resumed the classes I started after graduating high school. I wanted to finish with my friends but being a young mom and almost 200 lbs. overweight, I was not able to give it my all. I was too distracted by home events and the fact that I didn't seem to fit in with everyone else. But this time around, I was determined to finish what I started no matter what challenges were tossed my way. I then set a new goal for myself, I wanted to finish at the top of my graduating class, and I did just that. I worked hard and managed to graduate with honors. And, although I'm proud of my accomplishments, it wasn't easy, mainly, due to me going through a divorce and having to go from being a stay-at-home mom to a single mom. Being a single mom was tough, it was fun, and it was easily the one thing that made me stay focused and accomplish my goals.

When I decided to end my marriage, I told my then husband that I wouldn't contest the divorce and fight for alimony or the family home if he agreed to give me full custody of our daughter. He agreed, so we moved into a cute apartment about five minutes away from his home. She and I were two peas in a pod. She was my reason for waking up at 5:30 every morning, going to work at a local day care to work to ensure her world wasn't turned upside down too much. I knew going from being home with me every day to being with strangers would be too hard of a transition for her at the time. So, I made sure my work and school hours did not interfere with our time together. We spent our evenings at a local bookstore, allowing us time together to complete our homework while saving in our utility cost. I was a very efficient person as a single mom. My job at the daycare allowed me to cut the cost of our food bill, and as well, she was able to eat breakfast and snacks at daycare, lunch at school, and dinner at home or at a local pizza place that had a $3.99

all you can eat special. My daughter didn't mind. She still tells me how much she misses those days when it was just she and I at the bookstore having fun with me drinking burnt coffee and her finding new books to share with me like "I Spy". Those days hold such fond memories for the both of us and a time I wouldn't trade for anything in the world. Life was tough. I was abused, I was cheated on, I was stalked, but I continued to rise in the face of it all, and that is what I hope my story is able to do for you; give you a reason to continue to rise.

END

HEART DISEASE

It should not come to anyone's surprise that Black women battle with Heart Disease. In a Black woman's lifetime, she battles with heartbreak, heart attacks and heart disease. Her everyday surroundings are contributing factors. She puts everyone first before herself, years go by and she still works to keep her family a flout. Meanwhile, her heart is on a downward spiral toward her demise. Black women are very talented in the kitchen, and this is often the comfort in the family. The nutritional choices of a Black woman can easily put her in the category of heart disease along with other health problems. The lack of self-care and education on healthy living she becomes a victim just like her mother, grandmother, sisters, and aunts. Instead of accepting this disease, why don't we educate ourselves to do better?

Heart Disease develops from high blood pressure. This is usually more common within Black women compared to White women, "About 37% of Black women have high blood pressure." (Barnes, 2020) That's not it, "Hypertension also increases the risk of stroke and congestive heart failure" so more and more Black women are going down a dark path with their health and wellness. "The Black

129

community's obesity crisis is a symbol of just how at-risk this segment of the population is." (Barnes, 2020)

LUPUS

Statistics have proven that Black women are three times more likely to develop lupus than Caucasian women. You're probably reading this asking yourself or Google, what is Lupus? *"Lupus is a chronic autoimmune disease that can damage any part of the body (skin, joints and/or organs inside the body). Chronic means that the signs and symptoms tend to persist longer than six weeks and often for many years."* *(African Americans and Lupus, 2020) The* part of the body that is impacted by Lupus is the same part of the body that is designed to fight off viruses; this has a backfiring impact on the body. *"A person's immune system with lupus cannot tell the difference between these foreign invaders and your body's healthy tissues and goes after healthy tissue as well." (African Americans and Lupus, 2020) When* the body is on a downward spiral and the immune system is not functioning properly that is referred to as "*Flares*" and when a person is feeling good, that is called *"remission"*. Through all the rain there is sunshine that overtakes the clouds. *"I have Lupus, Lupus does not have me." (Contributing Author, Gittens, 2020)*

A Journal to Healing HERstory

by Xiomara E. Gittens

God, why is this happening to me? What is this? How can it be? Not AGAIN!!!!!! Tears fell from my eyes as I stood in front of the sink. I could barely look at myself in the mirror. Who is this person? She looks nothing like me. My head was swollen almost three times its normal size; the scabs burned and itched as they continued to ooze from my scalp. My hands were swollen and bruised from all of the IV lines. My hair, my poor hair! How could something so innocent turn into a near death experience? I used natural products. I was doing everything right, or so I thought...

01.08.2018

"Dear Journal...

...Why did I get this journal? I'm not going to lie, I feel stupid. I'm technically talking to myself, right? Or am I talking to someone else?... I woke up feeling sore, I had pain. I am still trying to educate myself on lupus and autoimmune diseases in general. The past year has been very weird and uncomfortable, ups and downs, and like a complete rollercoaster. At some points I wanted to give up, but I thought about X'iera and her smile."

"Be kind to your mind, be patient with your body, walk boldly in your spirit."

-The Energy Nurse- Xiomara Elena

My name is Xiomara, I am the Energy Nurse and founder of The Purple Purpose. Before I go any further, let's go back to the beginning... When I was in the eighth grade, my left leg started to swell significantly. The doctors couldn't tell me what was happening; they barely had a diagnosis. After every lab and specialized test in the book, my primary care physician decided to send me to a specialist, where I was then diagnosed with lymph edema. I was able to live with that; at least, that was my plan. If you're wondering what lymph edema is, it is swelling of the lymph nodes. The ducts get blocked, and fluid starts to back up causing mild to severe swelling. I thought that I could handle this new diagnosis, until it was time to wear cute shoes and outfits. The swelling was so bad I could barely fit any of the latest trends. I started to doubt myself and became depressed and insecure about my appearance. I lived with what I thought was lymph edema until 2010, when my symptoms suddenly started to change.

October 2010....

I was in my sophomore year of college and I had become extremely sick. I had fevers, chills, pleurisy (fluid around the lungs), hallucinations, and was suffering from random moments of syncope (passing out or fainting). I tried my best to keep up with my work. This was my moment, the last semester of prerequisites before applying for the nursing program. My health started to get the best of me, and I had to withdraw from school. I went into a deep depression. My health has yet again, made its way to disturb my life. I didn't understand what was going on, and why it had to be me. I started to see a holistic doctor in Swedesboro, NJ. She was awesome, she taught me so much about my body, herbs, and healing. I started to feel well physically but was so confused and lost mentally. Little did I know, my life was about to take a drastic turn.

In November of 2010, I found out I was pregnant. Go figure, right? I was extremely sick and was just starting to recover. "Dang! What am I going to do? I am not even with my child's father. How will I do this?" Every thought crossed my mind, but I couldn't help but hold my belly and pray to God. He wouldn't give me anything I couldn't handle. I knew that this little bundle of joy deserved a chance. I knew it wasn't going to be an easy road, but I was willing to take on the job.

My pregnancy started off smooth, but by my second trimester, I started to notice a change. My feet started to swell, my body and joints started to ache, something felt off. My doctors started to see me once a week and referred me to maternal fetal medicine three times a week. I was now considered high risk. By the time I hit my third trimester I was having chest pain and I couldn't feel my baby kick. The doctors continued to monitor me three times a week. They called me to the office one day and told me that I had decreased fetal movement, related to the placenta being directly in the front. I got down on my knees, tears fled down my cheeks, as I prayed to God. I am protected, my baby is protected. I will give birth to a healthy child.

The Gift...

On July 7, 2011, I gave birth to a beautiful healthy baby girl. Giving birth is the most rewarding experience. How could I be so lucky to bring this angel into this world? I looked her in her eyes as she smiled back at me. "Hi, I'm your mommy." Flashing, bright lights shined in my eyes.

"Xio! Xio! Can you hear me?"

"Code, Code, get a doctor in here STAT!"

"Xio baby everything is going to be ok. Mommy is right here!"

I could hear all of these things, but I could feel myself going in and out. After giving birth, I had passed out due to excessive blood loss. I had to get two blood transfusions and was moved to another floor. Hours had gone by; it was now dark outside. I woke up looking for X'iera. I looked over, and there she was, wrapped in my mom's arms, swaddled so comfortably. When my mom placed her in my arms, I began to cry, holding her close and tight. You could've lost me, but God new you were special and needed your mommy. I love you. I promise I will never leave your side.

"I know that what I seek is also seeking me."

-Unknown

The Diagnosis...

Three years! Three years of feeling good and doing well. You had lost some weight, the swelling in your legs had gone down, you had started nursing school, but most importantly, you and X'iera were healthy and happy... And then boom.

October 6. 2014

"Grandpa, where are you? Call me back." That was the last message I left on your voicemail. I found myself picking my phone up every second, looking for a missed call or text message. I suddenly lost my appetite. It's been hours! HOURS! I called every local hospital, no luck. They had no patient by that name. We drove around looking for your car or some sort of sign. Suddenly my phone rang. I felt a knot in my throat as I stared at the number... It was the hospital. I answered hesitantly; a nice woman spoke on the other end of the line. She asked me to describe my grandfather again. She said that there was a man that may fit the description. She asked me if I was alone and told me to get there as soon as possible, and to drive safely...

On October 6, 2014 you transitioned, with no warning, no explanation, nothing. I was confused and hurt. I hurt deeply; the flashes of that night lingered for a very long time. I was heartbroken, and that hurt began to affect my mind, body, and spirit. I started to have pain all over my body, the episodes of syncope started to resurface, I started to see Black spots or "floaters", and I started to develop brain fog. Simple tasks started to become a struggle. Here we go again, another round of tests. I was referred to rheumatology, pulmonology, neurology, and cardiology. I was tested for every auto-immune disease, from lime's disease, multiple sclerosis, fibromyalgia, and lupus, just to name a few. In 2016, I was diagnosed with Systemic Lupus Erythematosus (SLE).

Treatment NO treatment...

You would think that actually having a diagnosis would help and bring some relief, right? You just get some medicine and take it to feel better. Well, that's the imagination. That's the picture they paint and advertise. For me, it was the exact opposite, instead it made things worse. I was on a lot of medication; I was prescribed steroid, anti-malaria, a medication that was used for chemotherapy patients, an antidepressant, NSAIDS, ADHD medication, and pain medication. After taking these medications every day, sometimes multiple times a day, my body started to feel different, my mood changed, new symptoms surfaced. I felt as though I was trying to find my way through a maze. This isn't treatment... This is torture...

The Allergic Reaction...

In October of 2017, I was in my third semester of nursing school. I had developed a routine and was excited to enter what I thought would be my LAST semester. I had decided to treat myself to some well overdue self-care and maintenance. I was going to get my hair dyed, cut, and styled. Prior to dying my hair, I made sure that the products were natural based. I felt like a whole new person! New me, who dis?

I enjoyed a girls' night out at the casino; it was long overdue. The next day, I worked on our class presentation with my group. I felt good, and I KNEW I looked good, but that didn't last. By the end of the night, I felt warmth from my head, like actual heat. I felt like one side of my forehead was tight and stiff, as if something was off. I looked in the mirror to discover a lump. A few hours later, my entire face felt hot, I had an extreme headache, and my hair was soaked with puss and drainage from lesions that covered my entire scalp. That "lump" had grown about twice its size. I immediately took Benadryl and drove myself to the emergency room.

After three emergency attempts, I was finally admitted into the hospital. I had a systemic infection, and my head was still swelling. I had serious facial edema, my scalp was covered with lesions, and I had a temperature... Here we go again...I was admitted for five days. I was put on antibiotics, steroids, muscle relaxers, and standard iv fluids. By the end of day three, things started to get better and by day five I was discharged home. A month later, I had cellulitis and was admitted into the hospital for another four days. I know what you're thinking, but I can't make this stuff up. I was tired, tired of being tired. I had to withdraw from nursing school AGAIN!

"I have Lupus, Lupus does not have me."

The Journey to Healing...

After the allergic reaction and cellulitis, I had decided to take a leap of faith. I was tired of taking meds every day; they were only making things worse. I decided to take myself off of every medication, and instead, treat myself natural and holistically. I started to feed my body more fruits and vegetables. I started exercising, doing yoga, meditating, taking herbal supplements and studying how to heal the body naturally. I started cleansing my space and journaling. I was surrounding myself around like-minded people with the same goals of healing. I fasted and detoxed, and manifested healing. Within one year, I was feeling and doing so much better.

"The test you fail, is the test you will see again."

A quote from my pastor Theodore Winsley.

I was given the same test, but different versions. They all occurred in or around October or involved traumatic health experiences. The last experience was a true eye opener, it was then I realized we have the power to heal ourselves. The more I fed my mind, body, and spirit the better I felt. The more I poured into my own cup, the more energized and charged I became. The more I spoke positivity and healing, the more I manifested healing. The more I grounded, the stronger I became. Healing is not linear... Every day I am healing, creating the highest, most healed version of myself.

The Purple Purpose: HERstory

2.28.18

"Dear Journal...

...I have decided to invest in my brand/organization, The Purple Purpose. I want to build a brand that helps individuals with autoimmune disease find their purpose, by mentoring, educating, and supporting them. Providing different services and opportunities for self-growth."

I created The Purple Purpose, using my personal experience, implementing the healing modalities I used to help me through my healing journey. I took my story to make HERstory. Healing starts from within, the trials and tribulations, the trauma, the ups and downs all help shape you and prepare you to show up in a different light. More healed, educated, and respected.

Close your eyes, place one hand over your belly and the other over your chest. Now, deeply inhale through your nose. And now exhale through your mouth. Imagine being at the beach alone, for each wave that comes to shore, deeply inhale and manifest everything you want for yourself. And for each wave that goes back out to sea, exhale and release everything that no longer serves you. Now inhale, let the air fill your chest, and now slowly exhale and release out through your mouth.

"I AM Healed...

I AM Capable...

I AM Strong...

I AM Fearless..."

Xoxo,

The Energy Nurse- Xiomara Elena

BREAST CANCER

The majority of Black women this day and age have had or knows someone who has been affected by breast cancer directly. Black women are more likely to die from breast cancer, *"White women's probability of dying from breast cancer is 1 in 37, while Black women's is 1 in 31."* *(Zahra Barnes, 2020)* Breast cancer is relatively aggressive so please every woman reading this go get checked. We as a community can hold each other accountable. By doing so, we can lower the risks significantly. There are benefits if you exercise, have a healthy diet, limit your alcohol intake, refrain from smoking, and self-examine yourself. Survivors walk past you every day. Here is one of those survivors strong enough to share her testimony.

No One Fights Alone

by Valerie Blackwell-Howard

Sitting in my favorite spot at home, drinking a hot cup of coffee, looking at the amazing scenery, spending my morning talking to God and thanking Him for blessing me to see and enjoy another Friday morning on this earth. My mind drifts back to that late evening in December 2017, when I felt a lump on my left breast while in the shower. Instantly afraid, I did not want to alarm my husband, because we both were looking forward to the wonderful trip to Paris that was scheduled in less than two and a half weeks after bringing in the New Year. Yes, I thought how blessed we were of this amazing gift from our daughter as we celebrated another year of marriage together; wow 30 years. A few days from now, we will be celebrating 33 years together as husband and wife.

But my mind keeps drifting to that early morning telephone call that I had with my breast doctor in January 2018: "Mrs. Howard we are calling to inform you that your test results came back positive; you have Breast Cancer. You need to schedule an appointment immediately. As I sat there trying to decide should I scream, cry, or yell, a quiet voice within me told me to just pray and be still. Through my prayer, I heard God's voice telling me, "Do not be afraid, for I am with you. You will have to go through this season in your life but know that I am with you." After hearing these words from God, I picked up the phone and told my husband to come home immediately, because I did not want to share this news with him over the phone.

But as I fast forward to my morning worship with God today, my thoughts are on the television series called "Survivors", which is seen by over 50 million Americans a week. The object of the game is that several players compete against each other as they try to survive in unknown territory. The last person standing wins the grand prize. But what is a survivor? We know that there are all kinds of survivors, survivors of abusive relationships, cancer survivors, and natural disaster survivors. The list goes on and on. However, the dictionary has several definitions. First, a person who copes well with difficulty is a survivor. Second, the remainder of the group, the last man standing is a survivor. Lastly, a survivor is a person who survives, especially a person remaining alive after an event in which others have died.

In the Bible, there is no mention of survivors, but it does use the word "overcomer". The root word for overcome has a very interesting meaning. In the original Greek, it means to prevail, to pass over to gain the victory. In the Bible, John 16:33 states, "These things I have spoken unto you, that in me ye might have peace. In the world ye shall have tribulation: but be of good cheer; I have overcome the world. 1 John 5:4 also states "For whatsoever is born of God overcometh the world: and this is the victory that overcometh the world, even our faith. God has provided a way for the Believer to be victorious over every foe we face. I am determined by my faith in our Heavenly Father that I am not only going to be a Survivor of this terrible disease, but I will be an "Overcomer" and that God will get the victory.

Yes, I was petrified when I received the call from my breast doctor. My anxiety level was high, and I was horror-stricken not knowing what would happen to me. I prayed and asked God why me, but all he replied to me was Why Not You. I did not know what to expect or how my body will cope with this cancer. I was devastated and afraid, not only for myself as I looked back over my life to see what could have caused me to have cancer, but also for my husband and children because not only would I be fighting to stay alive, but I would have to look at their faces of despair. But when I looked into their eyes, I prayed that I saw love, hope, and faith because I knew I could and would not be able to fight this battle without them fighting alongside me.

During this season of my life, coping with a breast cancer diagnosis, I have learned that we may make our plans, but God determines our steps. I had to let go of self and learn to hold on to God. It is said that anyone can give up the fight, because it's the easiest thing in the world to do. But true strength is found when it seems like everything is falling apart and everyone has left your side, and everyone expects you to fall apart. But through faith, God gives you the courage to hold it all together.

I try not to think about my treatment days, as those thoughts invade my mind with unanswered questions. Will I survive? What will happen? Am I strong enough to get through this? Who will love my children and grandchild? Am I still and will I be the same woman as I was before this journey began? Will my husband still love me the same? What and how will I feel and look after going through treatment, chemotherapy, minor surgery for port, radiation, double mastectomy and reconstruction surgery for this dreaded disease? But I still remember that day in January 2018 when the world just stood still; everything just stopped. After arriving home from a beautiful week in Paris, France, I immediately got on the phone to set up an appointment with my doctor. While in Paris during our romantic late-night dinners, I told my husband about the lump I felt on my breast and told him as soon as we were back in the states that I would set-up an appointment.

Each individual breast cancer survivor has their own story. Here is a little of mine. All I remember at my first appointment is my doctor telling me "First things first, one day at a time, one step at a time. That is how I want you to handle everything that is happening at this very moment. Try not to think too hard or too quickly." She advised me that a breast cancer diagnosis will cause a wide range of feelings: Denial, guilt, helplessness and anxiety and fear, which are all normal. And she advised that I should make time to share my feelings with my doctors and family, because this is a stressful time. But even before setting up a plan to proceed, I was introduced to a team of doctors, who I met with my breast doctor surgeon. I met my plastic surgeon, oncologist, radiologist, nurse navigator and social worker who all provided support, and I can say I love them all for making this journey successful. No, I was not expecting to be diagnosed with Triple Negative Breast Cancer. That day on February 1, 2018 felt like I needed a Groundhog Day; let's do this all over again. I was in a daze as I looked at my husband and daughter, totally relying on them to remember what had been said, along with the pages of my diagnosis, the diagrams and possible treatments, some of which I didn't even remember receiving.

And then I went on to other testing, pet-scan, whole body bone scan to ensure that the cancer has not spread to any other body parts or organs. Next came an MRI, diagnostic mammogram and ultrasound on my left breast, and echocardiograms. Finally, after all my scheduled tests and procedures, came genetic testing, which came back negative for the cancer gene. I was thankful that I was able to endure all of the tests and procedures; However, the genetic testing was really important to me; I wanted to ensure that I would not pass this disease onto my daughter or granddaughter, because there was a family history of breast cancer in my family. My maternal grandmother and mom, who are now deceased, both had breast cancer but did not die from this terrible disease. My breast doctor explained to me that I have Triple Negative Breast Cancer, also called TNBC, which lacks estrogen receptors, progesterone receptors, and over expression of the growth protein HER2. Also, TNBC has no targeted treatment, so patients like me can only rely on surgery, chemotherapy and radiation. I decided to have surgery first, because I wanted the tumor removed before I began chemotherapy. I know others have chosen to proceed with Chemo first to see if the tumor will shrink, but as I indicated, I just wanted it to be gone. We scheduled my surgery for the first week of March for the removal of the tumor, removal of several lymph nodes to see if the cancer has spread, and I also opted for a Double Mastectomy (both breasts removed), because I was afraid to take any chance of it recurring in the right breast. After surgery, I was diagnosed with Stage 2, Triple Negative Breast Cancer.

I began Chemotherapy treatment three weeks after removal of my tumor. I can remember being so afraid to start my first chemo treatment after hearing about this poison. I heard cancer patients call it the Red Devil, due to its side effects and because its color is red. Thank God that my husband was with me every week for my sixteen weekly taxol/carboplatin injections, and after chemo twenty-eight straight days of radiation, all completed September 2018. Seven months later there was a plan for reconstruction surgery to be performed by my plastic surgeon. Chemo literally made me sleep the whole day, taking anti-nausea medication and unable to eat, because of the metallic side effect of chemo treatment. And yes, there is also such a thing called chemo-brain, where I could not think clearly and had memory problems that occur sometimes during and even years after treatment. I just wanted to vent, feeling dreadful and ugly with my cancer during chemo. I lost all of my hair, but thankfully it has grown back. I was so desperate to feel like me again. It was hard to handle the changes and feelings; I just wanted to be normal and feel like I was back in charge of my life, because on most days it felt like cancer was in charge. I learned that I could change and take control over my life, and that I am no longer at the mercy of cancer.

Being diagnosed with breast cancer or any type of cancer will leave you terrified and feeling alone. No one can really know how you feel unless they are going through this same journey. It is just something that is unexplainable, as many cancer patients believe this is the end of the rope and that they need to get their affairs in order. I was terrified and had many feelings of being alone. Note to self: Many family and friends will not be able to go through or handle going through this journey with you, as I believe they just do not know how to comfort you or understand what is happening to your body, mind and spirit. I was excited that during my journey, I found out about a conference in Philadelphia, hosted by Living Beyond Breast Cancer Foundation. There I met members of the Triple Negative Breast Cancer community where they all came together to learn from experts and to connect with others facing the same disease. This is a sisterhood, which I am glad that I am a part of, but you really do not want to join or be a part of; however, this conference and organization came into my life at the perfect time in my life; it kept me sane and from feeling alone, because I thought no one could really understand my emotions. I decided to attend this three-day weekend event and it was there that I connected with the Triple Negative Breast Cancer Foundation (TNBC) for the first time. TNBC was born out of the love for a young mother. Nancy Block Zenna lost her battle with breast cancer and this foundation is her legacy, which is organized by some truly amazing women to ensure that No Breast Cancer Patient Fights This Battle Alone. Not only do I have an incredible group of family and friends by my side, but I also have this organization and many others, including Touch, The Black Breast Cancer Alliance run by my breastie and friend Ricki Fairley (CEO), where there is a push to eradicate Black breast cancer, because it is so devastating for Black women, all standing behind me and other women just like me as we continue to fight and raise awareness for TNBC.

In April of 2019, when I received a phone called from Hayley Dinerman, Executive Director and Annie Rogers Hausmann, two amazing women and friends of this amazing organization advised me that I was being recognized by the TNBC Foundation for their Courage Award. I was so overwhelmed. I thought at first that there were so many other women so much more deserving of this award, and who showed that they were so much more courageous than me. But she convinced me that I was deserving, and that I was an example of someone facing this disease with courage and grace. So many other women at the conference should have received this award, but I am forever thankful and blessed to have been selected for such an award, and I was so honored to represent the Triple Negative Breast Cancer community and was thankful for this opportunity.

Having cancer has given me a different perspective on life. Life after having cancer and not knowing if it may return again, has taught me that I do not want to spend my days worrying about whether this disease will reoccur, but I would rather spend my days sharing God's unconditional love with others, because there is nothing on this earth that is more important than the love of God. I am grateful that God has healed me physically from cancer, but even more important is that he has also healed me spiritually. God has shown me that I could trust Him with my life, because he controls everyone and all things, and that he is the only way to eternal life.

I leave you with this final verse from Deuteronomy 31:7-8, which I read every day: "Be strong and of a good courage, and the Lord, he it is that doth go before thee; He will be with thee, He will not fail thee, neither forsake thee, fear not, neither be dismayed".

END

SEXUALLY TRANSMITTED DISEASE

Dear Black Woman,

Stop trusting a man or a woman's word! Go get checked! As much as you might believe the individual, don't neglect common sense. As Black women, why do we lead in having the most sexually transmitted diseases, but yet we are the least likely to get married out of all race women? "Black women still outpace other groups when it comes to new diagnoses of these diseases, along with new diagnoses of syphilis, this problem also extends to HIV/AIDS." (Barnes, 2017) Why do men often choose to marry a woman other than the Black woman? Studies prove Black women hold one of the highest HIV/AIDS diagnoses, "Besides Black men, Black women comprise a majority of new HIV/AIDS diagnoses per year."

Why Black women, why? Why do we not realize our worth? Why do we refuse to put a stop to this! As Black women, let's put an end to ignoring the facts, "According, in 2015, 4,524 Black women were diagnosed with HIV in the United States, while 1,431 White women and 1,131 Hispanic/Latina women received the same diagnosis." (Barnes, 2017) BLACK WOMAN, ENOUGH IS ENOUGH! Let's not sit back and ignore the facts. We can come together and help educate one another on the health care issues and research preventative care that can help eliminate these issues. If we all pull together and come up with ways to better help the next woman, we can save so many lives. Other women oftentimes are accessible to more health care options, "Other women could see health care providers on a regular basis and be educated about what they should be doing to take care of themselves, and we probably wouldn't have as much of a problem."

Community economic imbalance continues to play a large role in Black women's health care. We as a community need to take responsibility for our minds, bodies, and spirits. Take women's lives as an example. Learn from the women who came before you and have been courageous enough to share their stories "There's a stigma around talking about sex, so people engage in risky sexual activity without protection." (Barnes, 2017) You don't have to take the hard road. So many women before you have gone down that path and they have shared their stories to advise you, although their children are gifts from God the road traveled is a dead-end street, "He was cute, I liked him, he pursued me, so we started having, poorly protected, ill-informed, adolescent sex. I got pregnant the very first time." (Tricoche, 2020)

PREMATURE DELIVERY

Countless Black lives are thrown away like paper towels. *We Rise* is not a cry but a scream for change! We deserve equal health care as any other race. Color shouldn't be the deciding factor of a person's worth. Enough is enough! Black mothers should be cared for with hast just like all other race mothers. It is clear that society doesn't agree that all lives matter. Black babies breathe the same air as White babies. Black mothers have contractions just like White mothers. So why does society continue to brush off Black mothers. We aren't cattle. Sojourner Truth "Ain't I a Woman?" Targets are already on standby to be slapped on the backs of Black babies. BLACK MOTHERS MATTER!

Giving birth to a premature baby can be extremely dangerous. What is the definition of premature? It has been defined as, "Giving birth prematurely, or going into labor before 37 weeks of pregnancy, can predispose a child to breathing issues, digestive problems, brain bleeding, and long-term developmental delays. It can also lead to death—the earlier a baby is born, the higher this danger becomes." (Gittens, 2020) So many Black children are born into a world that writes them off before ever letting them take their first breath, "Doctors said I was dangerously premature. They also went on to explain how abnormal of a case this was. The medical physicians went on to advise my mom to start praying because the chances were slim for her newborn baby to survive. My mother was faced with the scary reality that if her baby was to pull through that she would never walk, talk, or live a normal life." (Jasmine Poole, 2020) Sadly, Black women are particularly susceptible to giving birth to their unborn child early, "According to the CDC, the 2015 preterm birth rate in Black women was 13 percent; for White women it was 9 percent." (Barnes, 2017)

Factors such as high stress, unhealthy diet, obesity and teen pregnancy and the limited access to proper prenatal care all take ownership when it comes to premature labor. "My pregnancy started off smooth, but by my second trimester I started to notice a change. My feet started to swell, my body and joints started to ache, something felt off. My doctors started to see me once a week and referred me to maternal fetal medicine three times a week. I was now considered high risk. By the time I hit my third trimester I was having chest pain and I couldn't feel my baby kick. The doctors continued to monitor me three times a week. They called me to the office one day and told me that I had decreased fetal movement, related to the placenta being directly in the front. I got down on my knees, tears fled down my cheeks, as I prayed to God. I am protected, my baby is protected. I will give birth to a healthy child." (Gittens, 2020)

So often, socioeconomic setbacks plow into the lives of these Black pregnant women's lives that it makes it even harder to have a traditional pre delivery, "However, the CDC's Division of Reproductive Health is working on a variety of state and national level initiatives to reduce preterm birth in all women." (Barnes, 2017)

"Don't you realize that your body is the temple of the Holy Spirit, who lives in you and was given to you by God? You do not belong to yourself"
1 Corinthians 6:19

Below is a chart that summarizes many of the foods that have been researched and and have been proven to impact as disease-fighting foods.

Food/Beverages	Human Dose	Disease
Cherry Tomatoes	8 Cups uncooked per day	Systemic Lupus Erythematosus
Fish/shellfish high in PUFAs	3 ounces per day	Breast Cancer Colorectal Cancer
Olive Oil	3-4 tablespoons per day	Breast Cancer
Soy Milk	1 cup per day	Breast Cancer Atherosclerosis
Whole Wheat	2.7 servings per day	Cardiovascular Disease Type 2 Diabetes
Yogurt	1 Serving per day	Cardiovascular Disease
Apples	1-2 per day	Bladder Cancer Colorectal Cancer
Apricots	2 fruits per day	Esophageal Cancer Head & Neck

		Cancer
Black Tea	2 cups per day	Hypertension
Blackberries	5 ½ cups per day	Bladder Cancer
Blueberries	1 cup per week	Breast Cancer
Broccoli	1-2 cups per week	Breast Cancer Esophageal Cancer
Cashews	26 nuts per day	Colorectal Cancer
Sardines	1+ servings per week	Age-related macular regeneration
Red Wine	1 glass per day	Colorectal Cancer Atherosclerosis
Plums	2 fruits per day	Esophageal Cancer Head & Neck Cancer
Salmon	1 + serving per week	Age-Related Macular Degeneration
Green Tea	2-3 cups per day	Colorectal Cancer Cardiovascular Disease
Dark Meat Chicken	1 drumstick/thigh 100 grams) per day	Colorectal Cancer
Coffee	2+cups per day	Myocardial Infarction

Chart By: Eat to Beat Disease

WE RISE

4
Education

Ruby Bridges and federal escort as she integrated an elementary school.

Education Timeline for Black Women

1700's - 1800's

All throughout history, Black people were taught to fear learning, but it was never because Black people were incapable. It was due to the fact that earlier on in history the powerful realized that the key to empowerment was literacy. It was a simple method created by the White masters to keep the Black slaves dependent and illiterate so they would have to depend on their masters. Many slaves knew that literacy was independence, and knowledge was the door to freedom. "Stories were like a key unlocking a door." (Welch, 2000) So many southern states in the early

1700s have passed laws to make it illegal for Blacks to educate themselves. An example of this took place in the year 1740; South Carolina enacted a law making it illegal for slaves to be taught how to read and write. Nevertheless, African Americans ran into serious issues with literacy restrictions making it nearly impossible to better oneself due to the barriers designed to keep Blacks back. White American leaders thought that if you keep a person enslaved and illiterate, it would keep them dependent and not independent. In the year 1833, the Alabama Slave Code was set in place which included the following law "[S31] Any person who shall attempt to teach any free person of color, or slave, to spell, read or write, shall upon conviction thereof by indictment, be fined in a sum of not less than two hundred fifty dollars, nor more than five hundred dollars."

In the early 1870's, a system known as sharecropping came crashing down in most southern states. Sharecropping was an economic system to keep slaves who had just been freed from bondage. While many slaves often fled to the north, thousands stayed behind and became sharecroppers. Working the fields of their former White masters, sharecroppers were stuck in an endless cycle: Blacks would be given a small plot of farmland to work, and they would in return have to work sunup to sundown just to receive enough money for food and housing. Survival came first, and getting an education was not the priority for Black people "Most of the children get their schooling after the "crops are laid by," and very few there are that stay in school after the spring work has begun." (Welch, 2000)

As laws were being put in place to keep Black women back, there were organizations working twice as hard to break down those walls put in place to keep us back. Black women were expected to cook and take care of the children and house, but some women made sure they did everything in their power to educate themselves. Ida B. Wells-Barnett was a Black woman born into slavery, but she never was a slave because slavery ended shortly after she was born. Ida was a sharecropper who was raised by a Black mother who understood the importance of education, so Ida's mother pushed herself and her children to get a good education no matter what, "After the Civil War, many Black people - both children and adults--attended school for the first time. India's mother went to school with her children." (Welch, 2000) Women like Ida B. Wells-Barnett created the path for more Black women to pursue getting an education.

Throughout this time period, it was evident that the more Black women became educated, the more the walls that were built to keep Black women left behind started to come down. One of the most historical demonstrations of this happened in the year 1881. In Atlanta Georgia in the year of 1881 the first private, liberal arts, African American women's college was established, "The all-women's school was named after Laura Spelman Rockefeller, the daughter of an anti-slavery activists." (Taylor,2020)

Early 1900's-1950

Soon after the Historically Black College University (HBCU) era founded a new era that established not only the start of Black higher academics "Spelman women, as with many HBCU students, held a significant presence in the civil rights movement. In 1960, students were arrested for protest during a sit-in in downtown Atlanta." (Taylor, 2020)

This was the beginning of Black social groups "Greek life", meaning Black Greek-letter organizations. Greek life became one of the networking support groups for Black men and women in college. These Black fraternities and sororities (from the Latin words frater and soror, meaning "brother" and "sister" respectively) are fraternal social organizations for undergraduate students oftentimes. Greek life is oftentimes known for the brotherhood and sisterhood that these groups create within the Black community. (Greek, 2012)

In the Black community, Greek life is viewed as a positive networking and empowering group of people. These groups were founded in the early 1900's at a time when the world was beginning to further create ways to segregate Blacks and keep Black people divided. These African American Greek organizations understood and still understand the importance of community outreach and coming together. Greek organization members use these platforms as many different resources, one major one being, networking platforms that help one another in their careers.

Even with Black education on the rise in the early 1900's, America still was far from equal. Segregation was still alive all throughout the country and in the mid 1950's many African Americans at that time thought it was time to desegregate schools. This was a major turning point that took place on December 9, 1952 and went all the way until May 17, 1954 this moment was called "Brown vs. Board." This became a historical moment for all Americans. Education in America changed forever in Topeka Kansas in 1954 after the Supreme Court case in which the justices ruled unanimously that racial segregation of children in public schools was unconstitutional.

Who knew that a 6-year-old little girl would be the one to walk an entire nation into its destiny? A little girl by the name of Ruby Bridges became the bridge for Black and White students to cross together and integrate public schools. She was the first student to integrate segregated schools in America. In 1959, she attended a New Orleans kindergarten. Because of her courageousness our ancestors' wildest dreams came true. The time had finally come when desegregation finally was passed. That was a major turning point in America forever. Between the 1960's and 1970's, Black women were beginning to excel in acquiring higher education. In fact, oftentimes Black women would aspire to reach higher heights in education, so they didn't have to depend on a man to support them. Coretta Scott King once supported working and educated Black women by stating the following, "If you get an education and try to be somebody, you won't have to depend on anyone-not even a man." (King, 2017) Coretta Scott King and civil rights movement groups weren't the only ones who supported the notion of an educated Black woman.

Other groups such as the Community Empowerment Black Panthers in the mid 1970's were beginning to flourish in getting the Black women educated by implementing education platforms locally for Black people to attend. They were called "Saturday Liberation School" (Assata Shakur, 1987) After a long decade of organizing, protesting, and putting to action these educational systems, the Black woman was still pushed down by the world, which didn't always agree that Black women should acquire an education past a certain point. As we Black women left the 1970's and into the 1980's - 1990's, studies have proven that there is a population pattern reverting the change of desegregation and studies show that demographic residential tenancy highlight the fact segregation still lives by splitting communities by color. All the way through the 1980's into the 1990's, many people would say that the new generation of Black women during the 1990's was not seeking higher education like in previous years. Many people pose the question why is that? After all the hard work and sacrifice of the women who came before the new-school millennials, why don't more women take advantage of the current times? It almost seems as if many women are going backwards instead of forward. The classrooms expanded internationally. This new era of learning has tracked an entire generation of children. Doctors and medical professionals have misdiagnosed and overmedicated children. More jails have been renovated and expanded to accommodate the masses of incarceration. Still yet studies from the early 2000's have been buried so far leaving communities lost and uneducated. For example, in the early 2000's there was a study done in elementary schools with students to determine how many jails should be built. These are all hidden truths to continue a cycle of uneducated dependent people. The timeline of Black historic groundbreakers made the path for Black women to be anything they dedicated themselves to be. Nobody says the path isn't rocky but the more we explore new careers and further our education the smoother the path gets for the next generation following behind you.

"A lot of the Black kids had been put into remedial or what we called "dumb" classes. It never ceased to amaze me that the kids who were so smart in the street were always in dumb classes." (Assasta Shakur, 1987)

Scream Image

Elizabeth Eckford, one of the Little Rock Nine on her first day attending an integrated school. Hazel can be seen behind her in the crowd screaming. Little Rock Arkansas

EDUCATION

In society this day and age, it is a strong claim that Black women are the most educated in America. This study was confirmed after a study done in 2014. Black women have been found to be more enrolled in college more than any other race-gender groups. Yet despite Black women earning degrees more and more the negative imagery of the Black women still linger near, *"Images of the "welfare queen," "baby mama," and "angry Black woman," among other images, shame working-class Black women's struggles and reduce Black women's complex humanity."* (Katz 2020)

Achieving in the Wake of Adversity

by Kendiel A. Dorvilier, J.D.

As Black women, we know all too well the minor sense of apprehension that comes with changing hairstyles and returning to a predominantly White office or classroom. Will my colleagues stare? Will they make comments? Will I have to explain the installation process or justify why I sat for eight hours to have my hair braided?

During my first semester of law school, this was my plight. I started the school year off in mid-August with a sew-in. I'm not great at laying my edges or sticking to a strict relaxer regimen, so I thought these Italian-Yaki bundles would be a great, natural-looking style for a month or two. But by mid-October, I was ready for a change. Over fall break, I opted for an even more low-maintenance look – box braids, a classic go-to style for Black women.

When I returned from the long weekend, I received lots of compliments on my new hair. As my final class of the day ended, everybody started filing out of the lecture hall. A classmate of mine, who happens to be a White male, walked by me and said, "Wow, Kendeil. I don't know how I'm going to be able to tell you apart from the other girl in our class." Unsure of what exactly he was talking about, I asked him to clarify. With a smirk, he responded, "You know . . . the other girl with braids and glasses." At that moment, it was clear to me that he was referring to the only other Black woman in a lecture hall of 90 students. When applying to law school, I was well aware that I would be joining the legal profession as an underrepresented minority; I recognized my background was unlike most of my classmates'. Walking into any room, usually as the only Black woman, I knew that I had this superpower of being able to feel both invisible and hyper-visible at the same time. Still, for some reason, this interaction served as a stark reminder of those facts, and it stuck with me throughout the rest of my time at law school.

Since I was fifteen years old, I've held part-time jobs at theme parks, fast food restaurants, and everywhere in between. Throughout my undergraduate studies, I matriculated as a full-time student on an accelerated degree path, while also working full-time, 45-hours a week. While this experience certainly was not easy, it compelled me to become better at prioritizing, adapting, and asking for help when I needed it. With these skills and the guidance of several mentors (A/K/A my "Board of Trustees"), I was able to submit a top-ranking honors thesis paper on corporate fraud, which I later defended at a research symposium in Midtown Manhattan. I completed my accounting program with a 4.0 GPA. Moreover, I received scholarship offers of varying amounts to attend law school. Once in law school, I enrolled in a joint-degree, JD/MBA program. My credentials checked out. I deserved to be in any lecture hall or court room just as much as any other law student. But this didn't stop me from feeling small in certain rooms and situations.

The first year of law school was tough in that regard. I am a first-generation Haitian-American, raised in a small, low-income neighborhood by my miracle-working, single mother. I was the first in my immediate family to complete my bachelor's degree at a four-year institution and the first to pursue a graduate degree. While some of my colleagues were legacy law students, who came from a line of attorneys, I didn't know too many White-collar professionals, let alone legal professionals. Other colleagues of mine spent their Friday evenings in study groups at the library, reviewing the nuances of the Model Penal Code, mastering the rule against perpetuities, and quizzing each other on the Federal Rules of Civil Procedure. I spent mine traveling up and down routes 76, 95, 287, and 78, visiting my sister at a state prison in northern New Jersey.

The drive up to the facility usually took two hours. I'd get there early, wait in my car for the officers to begin the maximum-security visitors' registration process, and then I'd wait some more for the other visitors to check-in. No phones are allowed at the facility, so I would leave mine in my glove compartment and leave my keys in an on-site locker for 50 cents. Once a sizable group checked in, all of the visitors would load on to a New Jersey Department of Corrections school bus, for a quick ride to a multi-purpose building where they host visits.

Outside of the prison setting and the correctional officers supervising us behind a two-way mirror, it's all pretty regular for a moment. My sister would greet me with a longer-than-life hug, and we'd sit across from each other on a super uncomfortable picnic table made of silver steel. We would chat about everything under the sun: my jobs and internships; her part-time jobs; certain TV shows we've watched; new Cardi B songs that neither of us knew the names of or words to, but enjoyed, nonetheless. We'd talk about each other's hair textures, nail colors, and new recipes we've been trying out; and we'd stroll down memory lane. Some days, we'd even pose for a picture or two. All-in-all, we kept our visits light, laughing the whole time. Despite that, after hugging good-bye and boarding the bus once more to the front of the grounds, I always found myself leaving with my spirit feeling pretty heavy.

On the two-hour drive back, I usually rode in silence, trying to reconcile the duality of my experience—of my existence. On Monday through Friday, I sat in lectures that covered the ins-and-outs of criminal law and attending court hearings for course credit. On Friday night, however, I was sitting in a multi-purpose room at a prison with women whose cases were probably very similar to those featured in my criminal law textbook – an experience that many of my classmates may never have. I'd always think, what a blessing it must be to attend a homicide trial as a co-curricular activity, having no personal or otherwise vested interest in the outcome. A lot of these drives home were pretty discouraging. It took a few years of reflection to realize that, though I was differently situated than many of my peers, I was in a position to offer a perspective that most others could not. Quite frankly, finding strength in my struggles and owning, rather than running from, my story has been so empowering and monumental in my personal and professional growth.

That first semester of law school, I spent so much time trying to fit the mold of what a quintessential law student is known to be: always playing devil's advocate, focused solely on my studies, viewing my peers as my classroom competition rather than my future colleagues in the legal profession. I wasn't true to myself, my learning style, or my friendly disposition. And boy, did my grades reflect that. When first semester grades came out, I went from being a 4.0 student to a C-average student overnight. Of course, grading in law school is curved and confidential (meaning, the quality of your work is graded against the quality of your classmates'. Whoever has the better-sounding answer gets the better grade, and your answer and grade are bumped around accordingly). So, outside of my close friends and law firms I applied to for internships, nobody really knew how I did that first semester.

For this reason, I was a bit shocked at my classmates' reactions when I received a coveted job offer to work at a law firm immediately after my first year. It was as though my White counterparts assumed that I landed the role through one of the diversity programs designed to increase representation in the legal profession (note that roughly 5% of attorneys are Black). I should add that these diversity programs are highly competitive, and I only received one interview through this channel. It was as though I, a Black woman, could not possibly have competed with (and beat) them for a spot for which they were also being considered. For a while, I let these reactions get to me. Imposter syndrome crept in, whispering: Do you deserve this offer? Were you a mere diversity hire? Did they mean to pick you, or did they mistake you for "you know, the other girl with braids and glasses," in the interview lineup, who probably had better grades than you? How long until they find out that you're not as smart as they think you are?

During my second year of law school, I realized that these doubts were nothing more than imposter syndrome. When I received an offer to intern at an even larger, multinational firm after my second year of law school, I realized that I truly was exactly where I needed to be. (Alexa, play "Can't Tell Me Nothin'" by Kanye West). By my third year of law school, I made it a point to live my best life. I took classes that I enjoyed; I served as the President of my school's Black Law Students Association; I went out with my friends often, and still got my work done. In fact, even with these added responsibilities and activities, I saw a significant improvement in my academic performance. I worked hard and played harder.

Looking back, I realized that, when your grades or other benchmark won't get you into a room, maybe your work ethic, perseverance, personality, and grit will. Beyond getting into a room, these may take you further than you would ever imagine. Surely, new levels will come with new devils, challenges, and uncertainty. When faced with doubt or imposter syndrome, ask yourself, without a grade point average or a professional title, who am I? What do I value? What have I overcome? What sets me apart from my peers? What can I bring to the table? Am I built to last? Can I weather storms? Can I achieve in the wake of adversity? Of course, you can. And when you own this, you will be more powerful than you know.

Barbara Jordan helped lay the first foundation for Black women to become lawyers. Once one makes it, we all make it. Black women close race gaps each and every time they pursue higher education. Studies prove that Black women are some of the most educated and qualified women in the world. But yet, we are still paid less for the same job and less likely to be hired in the position you are more than qualified for. The Queen continues to strive towards greatness and educate yourself and never forget to help the next young lady who was once you. If we take a second to help the next queen, we will start to lessen the racial gaps.

"Knowledge is power. Information is liberation. Education is the premise of progress, in every society, in every family"

Kofi Annan

Built on the Rock, Not the Sandz

by Bianca Poole-Hill

Interest

After losing my two roommates and finishing a long and lonely first semester of college away from home, I finally found something that sparked my interest. A sisterhood that at the surface appeared to be for Black women making moves worldwide while still possessing high standards and class for themselves. After weeks of consuming myself with YouTube videos and books on Black Greek letter organizations, I was convinced that joining Alpha Kappa Alpha sorority was exactly what I needed to feel valuable on campus and get ahead in this White world.

Rush

After connecting with a few other young women that felt the same passion I did about joining the sorority, we collaborated on a plan to attend the first AKA rush hosted by our colleges in over three years. After going through hell and high water to get to the campus where the rush was being hosted, we were greeted by about eighty other young women with the dream. Completely intimidated by the poise and character of the women that held the "so -called" prestigious title of an Alpha Kappa Alpha woman, I yearned to become a member even more. After paying hundreds of dollars and going through a rollercoaster of a process to gain membership, I was one of only four women that were initiated that semester, soon learning that the real process was only just beginning.

Neophyte

After being formally initiated into the organization on a weekend getaway at a local hotel, I returned to the campus, full of excitement and ready to gloat in the glory of wearing those three prestigious letters. My new "sisters," and I immediately stocked up on paraphernalia, so it was not confused that we were proud members. As time went on, we quickly learned that there was a dark side to Greek life that we had no idea about but would soon learn. Our "neo" summer, we attended as many cookouts and events as we could in hopes of growing bonds with brothers and sisters in the organization and being known on our campus as well. Thinking back, my "line sister" and I in desperation, even taking a church van to a meet the Greek event on campus, were in way over our heads. As new members we stood out like green thumbs and were swiftly rejected by others that had joined the organization the dark way.

During that time, because of the rejection by others "so-called" sisters and Greek members, I was led to seek out the underground process of becoming a "so-called" real member. Soon after, connecting with a "sister" that was willing to share her underground process with my "line sister" and myself, we attempted to recreate the process ourselves in hopes of our neophytes not experiencing the shame and rejection we had. After being what we thought was enlightened about the true process, little did we know we were just digging a bigger hole for ourselves in the long run. We thought since we were the only Akas on our campus at the time, doing this would gain respect from other Greeks around the way. But instead, it turned us into around the way girls and soon after, I found myself pregnant and unsure who fathered my unborn child. At that point, I was faced with the decision to either drop out of nursing school and give up on my dreams of becoming a registered nurse or have an abortion. Being that I was unsure who the child's dad would have been, it made it easier on my conscience to make the decision to abort the child, a decision I regret until this day.

Riding Solo

That following fall semester, I found myself riding solo on campus as the only undergraduate member of AKA on both Bloomfield College campus and Montclair State University campus. My "line sister'' had transferred schools, and the dream of sisterhood I had once envisioned was now a distant memory full of dark scars. During that time, I was president and sole member of the AKA chapter at my school, still juggling chapter meetings, Greek council meetings on both campuses, and hosting campus events while still maintaining a course load as a nursing student. It was during this time that I realized nothing was as it seemed.

Growing Pains

I soon after found myself going to desperate measures to just belong. That following fall semester, I collaborated on a plan to find true sisterhood. At that time, I was deceived into believing this was my time to shine and finally make a name for myself. I pulled some young women that at the time seemed to stand out to me. I worked with others to develop a process to build what I thought would be a closer bond with these select women. They all consented without question, blinded by the same dream as me. Only one young lady had questioned the authenticity of the process and backed out towards the end. After they were initiated into the sorority formally, we built a bond like no other; they would do anything for me and vice versa. At this point, I was so caught up in the moment; I nearly failed out of nursing school, barely passing my classes that semester, not to mention the emotional and psychological torment I put those young ladies and others through, all for a moment of clout on campus. Although some skepticism arose around the campuses about what had transpired with our chapter, we all were closer than ever and refused to give in to what we perceived as people that were envious and hated our notoriety. These sisters had my back, and I had their backs no matter what. Soon after graduation we all began to live our own lives.

Reflections

After returning home from college, I woke up to the reality that once again sisterhood had become a fading memory that created new scars of regret and shame. However, this time I hurt even more people and lived with the guilt of it all on my shoulders, afraid that they may find out the truth. In late 2015, I got engaged to my on again off again boyfriend of seven years and this was the time Abba was purging me inside out. I got married six months after getting engaged, and during that time

I reconnected with my "sisters", one even being my bridesmaid. They were all so supportive and loved me so much that it seemed to be impossible to tell them the truth of what I did, and I just wanted to bury the issue. At this point, we all were out of college and I figured it did not matter anymore. But God had different plans for me.

Testimony

After my wedding, my husband and I had a double trip honeymoon planned to Jamaica followed by Las Vegas. However, three days into the honeymoon, my husband and I experienced a supernatural encounter that would change our lives forever. During that divine encounter I developed such a strong fear and reverence of God that my husband and I made the decision to end our honeymoon early while in Jamaica, and I spent the next seven days in a psychiatric hospital. It was during this time, I realized God was beginning to purge me of myself to become a vessel for his divine use. He was preparing me for something bigger than myself. At that time, I totally embraced the saying, *"embarrassment lasts for a moment, but regret lasts for a lifetime."* I began to realize that I had to do what was right and not what was easy, and that included telling the truth to my sisters and denouncing AKA. At the time, the fear of disappointing God was way more important than potentially losing the relationships that I had built with these women, so I told them all the truth. As expected, they were extremely upset with me, and rightfully so. I pleaded with them for forgiveness, attempting to explain that my dream of pleasing God was more important than living a lie for my own selfish gain. After eight years of the rollercoaster of Greek life, I publicly denounced membership to Alpha Kappa Alpha sorority by sending a notarized letter to headquarters corporate office, and posting my denouncement on social media, cutting all ties to the organization and Greek life as a whole. AKA and all Greek letter organizations were created to take the place of

God. Unfortunately, this is a lesson I had to learn the hard way, sacrificing a lot in the name of sisterhood, building my glass house on the sands.

Reflecting on all I have experienced, I have grown to understand that Yah's Will supersedes ours and will always be done. Every mistake I have made has only come to make my faith in my Savior Jesus stronger. I now live life looking for ways to help, inspire, and grow in the knowledge of Jesus our returning Messiah and share that with others in all that I do. The Bible says, "train up a child in the way they should go, and when they are old, they will not depart." I am living proof after going astray, Abba's grace was greater than my sin. My faith foundation through it all was always Jesus, my solid rock, never forgetting his blood covered all my sins. However, it was not until I humbled myself and repented that I could be used as a Vessel of Honor.

END

HBCU

There are 101 Historically Black Colleges and Universities. In 1837 The Institute for Colored Youth, became the first higher education institution for blacks, founded in Cheyney, Pennsylvania. HBCUs were established to create opportunities to African Americans especially down in the south. Prior to the Civil Rights movement in the 1960's HBCUs took on one of the only roles Black Americans could pursue higher education. Since then, HBCUs have spread throughout the United States. As of 2021 there are 101 Historically Black Colleges and Universities. HBCUs provide a stable and empowering educational environment. HBCUs offer many academic programs, diversity and welcoming student bodies, extremely supportive campus environments, and a unique learning experience. Many of these universities are designed to accommodate the students who are first generation college students, low income, or academically not prepared. HBCUs provide students with the richness of the entire college experience.

My Dreams Came True at an HBCU

By Rhonda M. Sessons, D.V.M.

My founding father is better than yours! This is a common form of teasing within the HBCU alumni community. If you are a generation Xer, like I am, you surely grew up watching some of these positive Black images in sitcoms on prime-time TV and may have envisioned, like I did, that college, especially an HBCU, is just like the TV show "A Different World", that we'd drop everything to watch on Thursday nights after the Cosby show and discussed among friends the next day in school. My gravitation toward an HBCU was evidently in my DNA, passed down to me from my mother who is a proud graduate of the oldest HBCU in the nation herself. I take great pride in telling anyone who asks, and anyone who doesn't, that I went to Tuskegee and promote and represent my alma mater unapologetically. The "Tuskegee Experience" is nothing short of spiritual to me, as an excellent education was not the only thing I left "Mother Tuskegee" with. The numerous priceless lessons I have learned (which I could write a novel about) continue to carry me through life and have made me into the person that I am today, for which I am eternally grateful. I know that I am only one voice of hundreds of thousands that can attest to this sentiment, but I will only tell my story for now.

I inhaled deeply while basking in the brilliant sun and taking it all in. The grass was almost an emerald green with that familiar fresh scent of a freshly mowed lawn. I immediately felt a peace come over my body as my heart made a leap in my chest, confirming that my decision was God's will. It was eight hundred miles from home, and I had never been that far from my family ever before, however a calm confidence filled my soul with a knowing that I was exactly where I was meant to be. I had made a decision that would change my life forever. I had been declaring to everyone around me during my entire senior year of high school that I would be going to Tuskegee University, even before I had applied and gotten accepted. Ha! And my, oh my, there is power in words; that's lesson number one! I could actually feel the history as I walked throughout the campus. Nearing the impressive monument located near the entrance, I stood there gazing at Mr. Booker Taliaferro Washington's statue, and while lifting the veil, he seemed to stare at me in the most welcoming yet challenging way as if to say, "I am pleased to have helped to make possible this opportunity for you, now what are you going to do with it?" Even at eighteen, I knew this would be a pivotal point in my life. Nonetheless, as a friendly, yet introverted teenager, living such a long distance from home for the first time in my life, was both exciting and scary. I now realized in that first week of my freshman year, that I would have to go out of my comfort zone and to seek out a way to throw myself fully into college life in some way. I had no idea how to do this; however, my independent nature reared itself when I saw a sign hanging up, among many, in the school student union after checking my mailbox that stated there would be auditions for the prestigious Tuskegee University Golden Voices Choir in the chapel the next day. Something stirred inside of me because I have always loved to sing and to be in a choir and would be a great activity outside of my studies that would effectively ease me into college life. The next evening, determined not to flake out on myself, I stepped out of my dorm room and walked over to the campus chapel alone. As I waited on the outside of the door to the choir room, nervous energy had me contemplating leaving and going back to my dorm after hearing the amazing voices coming from the other side when a friendly young woman standing in line in front of me turned around to me and asked "Hi, what's your name, where are you from?", in an adorable southern accent. I answered, "I'm Rhonda, from New Jersey, where are you from?" From there I learned her name and her hometown was Montgomery, Alabama. In those few minutes, I found her energy was fun and upbeat and I felt comfortable, so we agreed to go to the cafeteria for dinner after the auditions. Needless to say, I stayed, saying to myself that wasn't bad, I can do this, I can make friends. After successfully gaining acceptance into the choir, with a satisfying performance, I met a fellow alto named who similar to me, had a laid back but fun-loving demeanor. After a few jokes, we quickly clicked like we'd known each other all of our lives, bonded even more knowing that we had the same weird sense of humor and were from neighboring states! This is a big deal when you are from the North, and you live in the South. The three of us became fast friends and a steadfast trio who were always together. The adventures we shared for those four years were part of the unique experience that is life at a college that is an HBCU, it was a new world experiencing life at an HBCU in homecomings and trips to Atlanta, local southern eateries and getting used to grocery shopping in Piggly Wiggly, all within an HBCU environment. To this day we remain great friends, talking to each other regularly and participating in each other's major life events. Lesson number two, sometimes you must reach out into the unknown and push through your protective comfortable shell in order to experience life to the fullest and gain abundantly more joy than you could ever think or ask for in life.

Although I had quickly grown accustomed to college life, I was not exempt from the common problem that freshmen have of allowing idle distractions to affect academic performance. At the end of freshman year, remembering that my choice for Tuskegee was very strategic in that my end goal was always to attend and graduate from the extremely selective Tuskegee University School of Veterinary medicine, the only HBCU to have such, I had to make the hard but necessary decision to put my passion for singing and music on hold to focus on making my grades competitive for the veterinary school. I loved most of the choice of curriculums we had and professors that made school fun and interesting like none other kind of schools. They had the most character and boldness to keep it real with us. They taught us more about ourselves and our history more than any textbook could. Don't you dare believe that you don't learn about diversity here, that it's "not like the real world" that going to any HBCU is like living in a bubble. I learned more about diversity and other cultures and nationalities, races, and social environments there that I ever have before or since.

Attending Tuskegee to me felt oddly like being a child and getting to hang around all of my cousins during an infinitely long family reunion, if you can imagine, no matter the academic classification, social status or demographic background. Closer to graduation, the anticipation of a college degree was affirming to me. It was a boost of confidence to know that I achieved this milestone and that I can go on to achieve the next. Another perk of attending an HBCU is having influential public figures in the Black community as commencement speakers. The famous record producer, Quincy Jones, spoke at the graduation ceremony when I obtained my Bachelor's in Science that year. His daughter was graduating from vet school that year. Donning my cap and gown, I proudly took pride in my degree which was decorated with the distinctive Tuskegee logo with "Booker T" as we fondly, yet respectfully refer to our founding father, engraved on the piece of paper right next to my name. We are the elite, classified as one of the six Black Ivy League schools. I held my head high and stuck my chest out as if I had a "TU" on my chest like Superman has an "S". The statue of Booker T is the most sought-after photograph to get for every graduate and their family after the ceremony is over, and we were no exception. In that moment, not only did I feel like I made my family proud but also the smiling spirit of Booker T was "lifting the veil" off of me as my right of passage into the world.

Although I had spent all of my summers between academic calendar years, back in New Jersey, I had begun to regard Tuskegee as kind of like my second home. After freshman year, when I returned to New Jersey for the summer, I had frequently been told that I had picked up a slight southern accent! Who me!?! I definitely couldn't tell, I found it funny, nonetheless. I knew I had a challenging road ahead but obtaining that degree made me confident that I could handle a more intense schooling, a rigorous academic program and life for another four years in Alabama, and this time with my own car no less! Oh, I was invincible when I received that vet school acceptance letter. Both a whole new and "a different world" were waiting. Going to Tuskegee University School of Veterinary Medicine is almost like attending a whole different institution, but it was very clearly still a part of "the pride of the swift growing south." The social and academic climate was so different and yet extremely intense.

I had some of the best professors and swelled with pride having all of the African American and POC veterinary professionals teaching my classes. I was awestruck at some of the unique personalities some of my professors showed us daily, through their different forms of teaching, lightening the stress of learning the immense amount of material in that rigorous fast paced program that meant everything to our lives. I even still chuckle now at some of the things some have said but were important to things that make me remember key concepts in my professional career.

My first year of vet school proved to be absolutely strenuous. I thought I was ready, but I was not ready. The combination of my regular old reliable study habits from undergrad, having my own car, and having a boyfriend did not make for a successful year for me. My old ways of studying were in no way good enough for this demanding and fast paced veterinary medicine curriculum, and apparently, I was the last to find out. I must admit that I felt myself slipping down a slope and going into a hole as the second semester of my first year, came to a close, but I believed I would make it through somehow and go to the second year of vet school as assumed. I apparently was in denial. However, one spring day at the end of that semester, my designated slot to discuss my year-end review performance in the program with the program director and anatomy professor had come.

I entered the office to his stoic face as he greeted me by my first name as he always did. His demeanor was pleasant but serious. I greeted him in turn and sat down in the chair next to his desk. He began to tell me slowly, looking me in the eye, that based on my GPA, I would not be invited back to the next stage of the veterinary program in the fall. I had not made passing marks in two classes. Vet school only gets harder with each semester (a total of eight which equals four years); I was only on the second. After he finished, there was a silence. I looked down and away, instantly ashamed, with tears in my eyes, but I did not want to look like a big baby in front of this person that I respected so much. Not only had I felt like I let him down, but I let myself down as well and felt like a failure in that instant. Fat, salty tears landed on the thigh of my jeans. A lump appeared in my throat. My heart began to beat a million times faster.

My life seemed to flash before my eyes at that moment. I was mentally overcome with grief. Everything I had worked so hard for up until this point and done up until this point was for nothing. And I could blame no one but myself. These were words that no first-year vet student wants to hear. How could this happen? Why didn't I try harder? My pride had been in the way all my life honestly, it would not let me reach out for help or be open to doing things in a different way than what I was used to. My ego told me that I would still make it with the minimal effort I had made in undergraduate school, I took for granted by opportunity to achieve my goal. Although I had aspired to be a veterinarian since the age of 12, I did not take vet school seriously, once I was there.

The professor regarded me closely during the awkward silence. He observed how upset I was. He then asked me if I had any questions. I felt immediate shame and couldn't answer as I sat there in defeat, disbelief, and shock with a growing lump in my throat. Not trusting my voice, I remained silent. Then he looked at me (I still couldn't make eye contact) and gently told me with his thick Sudanese accent, "Rhonda, I know without a doubt that you will make a great veterinarian one day'" My world was shattering and for a second, his words didn't register as I sat there grieving my veterinary career in my head. Then I believe God jarred my spirit and allowed me to process what my professor had just said to me through my tears and pity party. At that point, I found the guts to lift my head up and look him in the eyes. Seeing his kind eyes and sincere countenance, my heart became unbroken in that instant. He was not just saying this to me. God spoke through him directly to my spirit in that office.

When I could finally find my voice (felt like forever), I replied, "Really?", desperately wanting to believe him and believe that there was still hope for me to become the veterinarian that I had so dreamed of becoming. He said yes and proceeded to inform me of the re-application process, where to start, how long it would take, what to expect etc. It sounded so daunting, and I doubted if I could go through all of that for a minute, self-doubt crept in and so did utter discouragement. But then those words echoed to me over and over and soon; hope returned. I took it all in through the tears. The shame I faced thinking of going to have to tell my parents I flunked out (might as well call it what it is!). I never flunked out of anything in my life! But there I was, kicked out of vet school the first day of May in 2000. I had previously been a high achieving hard working, focused and determined individual. Soon I realized I had to apply all of these skills into getting back into vet school.

I was depressed for the next few days. I finally got home and reluctantly told my mother who was very comforting and helped me through the complicated process of reapplying to the School of Veterinary Medicine at Tuskegee University. It was quite a humbling experience. It's like getting left back in grade school and it's like you no longer belong. The camaraderie of your previous classmates is gone, and you now must start all over with a class of strangers. Nevertheless, my efforts proved successful; I was accepted into the veterinary program one semester later to start with a brand-new class in which I knew no one. I soon found out that I was not in my boat alone. Another peer from my previous class ended up sitting with me repeating the same classes, also having been set back one year. Eventually God gave me a friend to form a study group with who had that same predicament, we were in the first class together, had also not made the grades to stay and had to reapply to get accepted just like I did. We stuck together and repeated the classes we didn't pass together and began a friendship, vet school study partnership and was each other's support system.

We remain good friends beyond Tuskegee and have kept in touch and traveled often together. I really can't tell you how embarrassed I was because now I was in the new class where I knew no one and probably looked at as the girl that flunked out of the second-year class. You know, it's like getting left back in grade school. My mom told me that I wasn't the first and sadly I more than likely wouldn't be the last. I was blessed to be accepted back in as many are not invited back into the program after that. I had to count my blessings and be grateful even though I wasn't where I wanted to be at that time in my life. We were each other's study group for the next three years and became lifelong friends. We bonded over that and became best study buddies and great friends. The awesome TU administration gave me another chance to be a TU alumnus for a second time. My performance really thrived the second time around. I even got straight A's in my second year.

This was nothing but God at work for which I take no credit. Thanking God for the awesome TU administration for giving me another chance to achieve my childhood dream and for the favor for being a TU alumnus. I didn't take this lightly. I had no more setbacks and graduated with a great GPA, not cum laude or magna cum laude, but still just as something to be proud of. It should have been a year earlier, but none of those matters 16 years later, the time of this writing. Do things always happen on our timetable? Unfortunately, (but many times, fortunately depending on how you view things) God has a plan for everything and everything happens for a reason. If I had not learned this lesson then, I may have had to learn it later in another situation at a most inopportune time. I have become a great veterinarian as my professor predicted. Even now, many years later, I still hear his voice in the back of my mind, speaking up when I begin to doubt myself. I have to admit, there was a time when part of me still didn't believe him and even assumed that I would be considered less than for acknowledging this setback in my life.

For years, I was embarrassed by this blemish on my past for a long time and never wanted to acknowledge my truth. Not giving up on my dream enabled me to accept that failure as a seed for my success. Resilience was my new superpower and giving up is never an option. However, as I grow in my career, I stay humbled by learning this lesson and my life has turned into a testimony to his words. That one encouraging sentence spoken by God through him, propelled me to accomplish my optimal goal of becoming a veterinarian. I love what I do and could never imagine doing anything else. His words were pivotal in the person I am today, especially as a veterinary professional. Not sure if my story would have gone that way at another veterinary school but "Mother Tuskegee" wanted nothing but for me to succeed and she made sure I got the lessons in order to be who I need to be in life by putting the finishing touches on entering adulthood.

The Tuskegee experience is a spiritual experience. It is a place where I learned fundamental lessons and swallowed my pride many times. But that was only the beginning as I am in a lifelong process of evolving, and a lesson in resilience is just one of many that you get without sitting in a class or reading a book. There are situations in our lives when determination coupled with persistence can take you a lot further in life than the cliché high IQ's or having "smarts" ever could. "'Skegee made me" is a popular social media hash tag among my many fellow alumni, for I have learned that failure is not the ending when you have a goal to achieve and the environment in which you surround yourself in while achieving your goals, makes all the difference. From then on, I would never doubt my ability to succeed, although it is important to remind yourself of this fact regularly. For me, going to Tuskegee is the best decision I have ever made. The experience, the people, the professors, the choir, the ups and the downs are forever etched fondly into my heart. I regret nothing and wouldn't change a thing, not even my failures. Tuskegee University is a world-renowned national treasure to which I am proudly forever linked. It is integral to my essence and is the inspiration behind most of my passions in life which shapes my identity.

HBCUs are important institutions of higher education especially for the Black community. Just ask any HBCU alumnus! You get to live, feel and see the history on campus daily. Everything you do see and hear is the direct influence of that great legacy. By attending an HBCU, not only did I get an excellent education that is world renowned, but I also learn about my Black history. For example, just ask any HBCU grad about being required to learn and be graded on every verse of the Black national anthem and learn about your place in the world in this life as well.

END

I Don't Break, I Bend

by Heavenly Odom

Life broke me but I wasn't broken. I never even knew I had a story to tell. I didn't ever think there was significance in my story. I think it's because for so long, I numbed myself to it all. The pain, the hurt, the disappointment, everything. For years on end, nothing ever bothered me or affected me. I was on autopilot. Until one day, it all came crashing down.

I've received many gifts in my lifetime; some I do not even own anymore. When you opened a gift, you would release an expression of emotion, usually happiness, joy, or contempt. In the time, I was privy to why I had received this gift because it caused more destruction than anything. This one particular gift that I would always remember was hurt – because the hurt actually healed me. Because in order to build something great, you may have to break a few things down. It almost got to the point of where I was broke – but it didn't break me.

For so long, I just lived. I wasn't alive but I was here. In the midst of not being able to feel, I still had the most compassion for others and less than minimal for myself. I thought I didn't need it for myself, I could just give it to the people around me.

I really struggled with identity issues most of my life. I felt like who I was wasn't enough for people to like, so I had to fit into their status quo. However, school came easily to me; that's the environment that tumbled with me the most. Did I fit in with the girls from the hood, or did I show I was said to be not "like that?"

I found myself hating that I was strong, because it's not like I had a choice to be. If it were a choice, then maybe I would appreciate the compliment. So many people saw things in me that I never saw in myself. Sure, I'm smart in school. Making it: Isn't that what was I supposed to do?

Nothing made sense to me until my pain revealed the magnitude of who I was.

For years on end, I went through an identity crisis. Never knew Who I should be or wanted to be, just rather who I felt I needed to be. Please believe me, the road wasn't easy. It was painful but I felt no pain.

Although I sided on being the most caring person to people around me and the happiest person, I was living in a world unknown, and I couldn't explain any of the feelings I had. There was a period of time that I completely do not recall. I remember maybe bits and pieces, but for the most part, it's vague.

I used to always wonder why I never felt. Even when it came to joy, it never felt like anything, until the moment it did. I think all my life I numbed myself to pain, because it was never ending. In fact, I couldn't feel pain, because I had to be strong. I was the oldest to my younger brother and sister who looked up to me. Daddy was locked up, and Mommy was killing the game on her own. So really, it was no time to stop and feel pain. Even when it hurt, you were fine, and you just had to keep going. Now that I think about it, that's really some toxic stuff.

I was given a surprise in 2017. Gifts usually came in colored boxes and wrapped with bows. But this gift came with tears and feelings. The gift was heartbreak. She was adorned with love; she even crept calmly on me. But the reason why she was a gift was because she made me feel awake and alive again. So, instead of the pain actually hurting me, it healed me.

I wouldn't say when the first gift came around. I got all my life together and everything was keen and perfect after. The only thing that changed was the ability to feel. Now, instead of no tears, all there was were tears. Instead of no smiles, there were smiles. I had gone through this change in front of the eyes of another person who could attest for it all. Every emotion was on a high and I was straight up feeling EVERYTHING. The good thing that came from it though, is she was kind of remembering all the past emotions.

At the moment that the gift came, I wasn't grateful or didn't welcome it with open arms. I questioned it, myself, and nearly everyone around me. It confused me, belittled me, and strung me out to dry. But to the world, nothing was nearly even wrong, but I felt a fire inside of me. The hurt healed me. After this gift, I now knew and was now aware. Maybe even cold, but sharper. It was no longer Mrs. Nice Guy and no longer the one to be taken advantage of from the people who warned me I gave too much.

I had so many broken parts of me but still the ability to heal others. People would feel good around me. They sensed this piece of peace around me that I didn't even know I had. In the midst of being broke, I made others feel whole. I connected my personal life to my professional life and for a while, they didn't seem to mingle. There was a point in time where I believed I was a vessel. I was divinely created to be used by others to help and heal them, and when I couldn't, I didn't belong. Absolutely nothing was wrong with it, except when you had nothing left to give, who was giving to you? Who was pouring into your cup?

My parents actively being on me in school and the strong desire, and will I had to learn more contributes to who I am today. Every day, I wanted to learn more. I was always intrigued as a student. A person who realizes they have learning to do, and always does is a person who will never stop learning. While I transitioned to where my destiny is now, I made a couple of pit stops. In fact, some of the pit stops I had were all revelations of my internal desire to help others. Lawyer's office. 911 Dispatcher. Banker. Tutor. During tutoring, I found an angel. Speaking to her was one of the most memorable moments in life for me because she managed to speak to my soul barely knowing me. She told me "you're a healer." I had no clue what that meant or even how to apply it. With just the knowledge that enjoyed people smiling around, that was good enough. Fast forward, she continued to adorn my spirit and even is the catalyst to who Heavenly is today. She coaxed and highly encouraged me to become an Educator. I brushed away the idea. Because she was a White woman, had White privilege, and everything White, I felt she had no idea what she was talking about. She would say "There's something in you. A fire. Your parents did well. I haven't met a lot of young Black women like you. You need to teach. But most importantly, not for you, for them. Those kids need to see people like YOU."

And that was it. I did it. I gave it a shot. Multiple times. Never was good at sports, so I missed a couple of times. But when I did make the basket, the crowd went wild. Who would've thought your girl would ever become a teacher? From wanting to be an OBGYN, mortician, etc., I had no inkling of teaching though, until I did. And now that cup that had been running dry and empty from those around me, was refilled and overflowing.

I wasn't meant to teach. I was meant to lead. I considered myself the Harriet Tubman of our time. The tool that I had was to not do the work for people, but to be able to relate to them for them to understand. That was my gift. Imagine 2+2=4. To some, I would say just that. But to others, I would say 3+1=4, and you still got the same result but from a different perspective. I had the keen ability to relate to others. So, whether it was the White girls from Morristown, they got the right answer, or whether it was the Black girls from Newark, they got the right answer.

I took on a huge project that might've been bigger than me, but I backed down from no completion. At the time, it didn't even seem like a big task – but it drained me, so I know for a fact it was. When I thought I was flawed with the ability to not feel, that was never the issue. I did feel. But I didn't mask my feelings, and this was what I wanted to teach. But at this particular project, we almost reached the finish line, but I had to give up because I could feel familiar signs and sounds of the same gift coming again. And I told myself, I would never let myself get back to a place I prayed out of. So, before the gift could come again – I backed out. Because now, she was feeling and feeling so much that it made her aware of everything around her and sharper than before.

There is strength in your struggle. And sometimes, we never know how strong we are until we have to be. Some days, I feel like I have been through hell and back, but I couldn't stop in Hell because that's not where I belonged.

A part of my journey of pain and hurt, I had no regrets; however, I needed a time out. Here I was fixing and leading others with no direction, filling others and not filling me. I told myself "Sis, it's time now – take a break, you need to relax." But before I stopped, I needed my credit. I had to name it. I was the Sun. I had the ability to bring light into darkens at any given moment. I could make you feel warm on the coldest day and I nurtured your soil so you could grow. But this time around, the Sun was dimming down. And not by choice. So, the choice was to let it go. The ability to let go was transformative. Because when I lost it, I found myself. When I thought I was breaking, I was only picking up the pieces.

Only now, the story isn't finished. I would be lying if I could finish or say this is the end when really, it's just the beginning. It's not that I couldn't feel pain before, but it was that I knew there was pain but really no need to acknowledge it.

My spiritual journey has awakened me and given me a new shape. All the experiences that I've been through were purposely divine and supposed to be mine. The pain was mine to have not hold. The love was mine to have not hold. If I couldn't handle it, it wouldn't have been given to me in the first place. While sometimes, I feel like I want to give up, I can't. Because my story is still being written and I have some more leading to do.

END

Children at early bookmobile mid 1900s

WE RISE

5

Position & Power

Get out to vote campaign

"The woman power of this nation can be the power which makes us whole and heals the rotten community, now shattered by war and poverty and racism I have great faith in the power of women who will dedicate themselves wholeheartedly to the task or remaking our society." (King, 2017)

What is a Black woman's position in America? Where do we fit in the scheme of things? If you ask the majority of us, we will say we don't fit anywhere in society. Black women come to the understanding that we were born into a world that never made a place for us to fit in, "As a Black person born into second -class citizenship and as a woman born into third - class citizenship." (King, 2017)

This leaves us to have to create our own place in this world. This difficult challenge never stops us from being trailblazers. In the early 1850's, one of the greatest Black women to lead by example in history went on a tour around the country to speak out about equality and Black rights. Her name was Sojourner Truth. Her voice was groundbreaking to the point it convicted many hearts who hated Blacks. In 1863, she became the first Black woman to be invited to the White House. After having met with President Lincoln, Truth helped get the Thirteenth Amendment passed, which freed the slaves. Truth's fight for women's right to vote in America will never be forgotten. Her speech "Ain't I a woman" made her a well-respected speaker and activist.

Sojourner Truth's courage to fight for equality for women did not stop after the Amendment passed; she continued to fight for the right to vote, "When the Voting Rights Act passed in 1965, fewer than 300 Blacks held major elected office in the United States. By 1972, there were 88 Black mayors, 140 judges, and magistrates, 13 congressmen, 246 state legislators, 740 city councilmen, and 675 school board members. Although those estimated 2,000 Black elected officials constituted 0.4% of the 521,760 elected officials in the United States overall." (King, 2017)

If it had not been for Sojourner Truth lifting her voice and using her power to bring forth change for women, there might not have ever been a Barbara Jordan. Barbara Jordan was the first Black woman to kick down the door for Black women in politics in Texas. Barbara was a Black woman who stood up to what most say is the most powerful man in the world. Barbara was one of the first Black women to prove the significance of having a seat in government, "As a member of the U.S. House of Representatives, Barbara was part of a special committee that had to decide whether to impeach President Richard Nixon." (McNair, 2000) It was Barbara's voice that made her so special, "The magic was there from the moment she opened her mouth.

Suddenly, she found a use for her special talent. She saw hope for African Americans looking to her for leadership. She knew what she had to do." (McNair, 2000) Blood, sweat and death was the cost hundreds of thousands of Black people had to endure just to get the chance to vote, "If Whites would kill a White woman for helping Blacks register to vote, I thought, what would they do to Blacks who attempted to vote?" (McNair, 2000) Just think about all the generations that paid the price just for us as Black women the chance to have a voice and vote, "The hands that picked cotton in 1964 will pick a president in 1972" Jesse Jackson once said. (King, 2017) As a community, so often we try our best to skip jury duty or neglect our duty to our ancestors to get out and vote, "It's a shame that too many Black people try to avoid jury duty, instead of trying to slow down the railroad." (Assata Shakur, 1987) There is no excuse in today's society not to cast your vote. There are unlimited resources and support groups that encourage Black people and especially Black women to go vote. Resources such as the NAACP, Movement Voter Project, Reclaim and countless more "Theory without practice is just as incomplete as practice without theory." (Assata Shakur, 1987) Instead of complaining about your community and remaining the victim, go vote "All you have to do is ask yourselves, who controls the government? And who are the victims of that control" (Assata Shakur, 1987) We have a voice, and it is our duty to vote not just for ourselves but our children and their children. In order to rid the corruptness, we must first register to vote and educate ourselves, "Everyone in jail isn't a criminal, and they've got a gang of criminals in the White House." (Assata Shakur, 1987) In the end, it is up to us to elect officials who will protect and serve us.

Power weighs heavily on a person's level of position. Black women have opinions, we have ideas, we are brilliant individuals that is why, and "We need more women in politics." (King, 2017)

"Any Black person in Amerika, if they are honest with themselves, have got to come to the conclusion that they don't know what it feels like to be free" (Assata Shakur, 1987)

It wasn't until 1920 that women in America were granted the right to vote. It is up to us as a people to use our voice and vote to bring forth the change needed for the next generation to come.

Coming Through it All

by Gaye Burton

On July 24, 2016, I accepted God as my Lord and Savior and rededicated my life to Christ. I was baptized with Holy water and took the bread as the body and the wine as the blood of Christ. That I might walk a more righteous life through my courses of action of repentance, love in my heart, and praising his holy name for the miracles cast in my life. Praising with humble thanksgiving for all my sunshine and rainy days in prayer and supplication unto Christ Jesus, Amen.

I was born and raised in the South Bronx of New York City. I come from a two-parent family and despite the fact that early in my life I lost part of my mother to a mental disease "Schizophrenia" and my father was there physically but unattached emotionally at times. My siblings and I survived without falling to crime, drugs or violence. I am the second oldest of five children. The first of my siblings to attend and finish college.

I got married and had children young. I started dating my husband at age 16 and he was 25 years old. Of course, he was my first love, became my husband and the father of my two sons. Unbeknownst to me, I was falling in love with a drug addict. The other dangers besides my husband's drug addiction were the fact that he had other bad habits. He was also a womanizer and he physically, mentally and emotionally abused me. Fear thou not; for I am with thee: be not dismayed; for I am thy God: I will strengthen thee; I will help thee; I will uphold thee with the right hand of my righteousness - Isaiah, 41:10 KJV.

Despite my fear of my husband, I refused to let him stop me from succeeding. I look back now, and I can't see how I made it through life, college and raised two good men. These horrific periods of my life could have broken me. Nevertheless, I obtained my Bachelor of Science degree in Elementary Education at City College of the City University of New York 1988. I received my first Master of Science degree in Special Education from City College of the City University of New York 1996.

But faith helped me to prevail and instead I suppressed these memories, I buried myself in loving, teaching and guiding my children, supporting my husband through his addiction, working, and finishing school and serving others. Faith revives me when I feel I can't take another poor day. For as the body without the spirit is dead, so faith without works is dead also - James, 2:26 KJV.

I have been an educator for twenty-five years. The first 2 years of teaching were under New York State and then I taught for 8 years in New York City Public schools. My first teaching experience was at a women's homeless shelter in New

York City as a preschool teacher in their day care center. It was there that I was reminded that I had a bigger job to do when it came to education. I felt the need to educate our youth and teach them the importance of getting an education and believing in themselves.

While teaching in the public school system it was also important to me to give back to my community. I wanted my students and parents to see me in additional roles in our community. So, I began my community service at a non-for-profit community center. I tutored and helped students with their homework and also taught GED English classes to adults. Because my oldest son attended this center, I felt the need to help organize and develop fundraisers as well.

When I moved from the west side of the Bronx to the South side of the Bronx, I gave back to this community as well. I maintained the position of the President and Resident Leader of the Tenants Association with South Bronx Churches and New Development and Vitalization Corp. It was soon after this commitment that I was approached by the district leader in my community to get involved with grass root actions to get the right leaders elected to office. I began to help by knocking on doors to secure signatures in order to get community leaders; and assembly men and women on ballots; canvassing neighborhoods to do literature drops and participating with phone bank calls from the board of elections. Although I had been voting since I was 18 years old it was at this time in my life when I truly realized just how important it was to vote.

Being a registered voter and getting involved in community service taught me that your community leaders are responsible to the people of their communities. I soon became a woman that wore many hats. I went from tutoring neighborhood students at a Tutorial Program to holding the office of President of the Democratic Club in the 79th District in the South Bronx. As if that weren't enough, I also became a youth leadership and community trainer for three summers. In this role I was responsible for training (17-21) year old youth about the Ella Baker and Cleveland Robinson philosophy of community leadership. Then in 1999, under the direction of Assemblywoman Gloria Davis and Bronx Supreme Court Judge Hansel McGee, I became part of a committee that wrote the grant proposal for the Harriet Tubman Charter School in the South Bronx that is still in existence today and has expanded.

During this time and after many years of abuse I sought a divorce. Before I could heal properly and get used to being a single parent, I was stalked by a man that lived in the building next door to mine. He terrorized me and my sons almost daily and the police did nothing about it. After two years of this terrifying ordeal, I decided to purchase a home and move to New Jersey to provide better living conditions and different opportunities for my family. Faith pulled me through a new life with much uncertainty. Consider it pure joy, my brothers, whenever you face trials of many kinds, because you know that the testing of your faith develops perseverance - James, 1:2-3 NIV.

My last fifteen years of teaching was as a Special Education teacher in Burlington County, New Jersey. When I arrived at the Middle School as a Special Education teacher, I was quickly recruited to join the district Minority Recruitment and Involvement Committee and our charge was to recruit minorities to become more actively involved in other committees under our local union association at the building level. My next role became the Middle School cheerleading coach which I did with joy. This role allowed me to mentor young girls to be role models, promote school pride, while maintaining good grades.

I did not stop there. I held many positions under the local association which included building representative; county representative and a county delegate to the National Education Association Assembly for eight years. These roles afforded me the opportunities to travel, sit in convention halls and vote on many legislative issues that affect public education. While serving in these roles I also maintained roles in my school building on committees in hopes of playing an intricate part in developing local and district goals to help promote high academic achievement among all learners.

I sat on and chaired many school building and district level professional committees. I also mentored students, teachers and trained other teachers as a facilitator. Each of these roles and commitments were important to me because they kept me abreast of many changes, challenges and it allowed me to take part in finding the solutions. In May 2012, I received my second Master of Science degree in Educational Leadership and Administration from Delaware Valley University in Doylestown, Pennsylvania.

However, due to unforeseen circumstances between the years 2012 and 2015 I went through a period where I suffered once again physically, mentally and emotionally. While I was trying to maintain my sanity, teach, wear many hats and complete school somehow, I became a target. I experienced being racially targeted, professionally harassed, discriminated against as my health and privacy rights were violated, and my character was attacked. It all started in 2012 when I had a parent harass me because I was her daughter's teacher. She tried to have me removed from the class simply because I was an African American woman.

When I expressed my feelings about not feeling supported by my peers in reference to this student's parents I was targeted by the administration. I was stripped of my physical accommodation. These were accommodations which were requested by my doctor and had already been honored previously. At the same time, I was dealing with another issue as a union representative. It was brought to my attention that there was an error in the teacher's schedule which violated the contract.

Right before the Christmas break, I was told that it would be recommended that my increment be taken away from me because I was late to work. My accommodation was supposed to protect me from these types of actions. This rough period also came about when I endured a fall while teaching in a classroom in 2013 which later resulted in severe back pain. Nonetheless being the fighter that I am in 2013, despite what I had just gone through I decided to run for the position of President of our local association.

I felt the strong need to pull our association together as there was a lot of decisiveness. The opposition at that time didn't want me to run for the position so she chose to get together with the administration to destroy me. The administration used their discontent along with the union representative actions to with-hold my increment and my local association did nothing to protect my rights. Instead, rumors were spread, and my personal medical information was disclosed to other members.

This was a clear violation of my HIPPA rights. While I did not win the election, I fought through this trying period in my life with my head held high and showed the school district what real integrity looks like. I eventually took matters into my own hands. At the end of the 2014-2015 school years, I was transferred to an elementary school. Then in April of 2015 I was accused by one of my students for stating that "I was going to kill myself because I couldn't deal with the children." Next thing I know I was on administrative leave and they were threatening to fire me. Of course, it was proved by a doctor that I was in my rightful state of mind. By faith I believe my Lord and Savior have carried me through each day, each struggle, each pain, and each lesson with resilience.

I decided to retire early because I feared for my job security. If I had gotten fired that would have prevented me from having the appropriate medical treatment for the injury I endured to my back. I left everything on the altar with God for his continued protection, healing, guidance and blessings in my life. I have been so blessed to understand who I am and whose I am. I worry at times, but I know I can do all things through Christ Jesus. I was suffering so badly from my back pain. I later found out that I needed surgery. I had surgery on March 16, 2016 and through God's grace I am much better. It was good for me to be afflicted so that I might learn your decrees - Psalm, 119: 71.

So, I continue to pay it forward even now during my retirement through volunteer work with the Township Alliance Group (TAG), which keeps residents informed about the risks, dangers, early detection and alcohol and drug prevention. I presently run a food pantry at my church, International revival Tabernacle. This position gives me the most joy and gratification. I am also a Pemberton Township Councilwoman. My charge here is to enforce government policy for the improvement of my community. My training and professional commitment as a community leader, advocator, teacher, trainer and a practicing Christian prepared me for this role.

But most of my pride comes from being a mother of two wonderful sons, and a grandmother of three beautiful granddaughters and the love of serving my Lord and Savior Jesus Christ! Faith sustained me through suffering pain. Faith assured me that I would be able to thrive after an early retirement. Lord, all my desires are before thee, and my groaning is not hid from thee - Psalm, 38:9 KJV. None of this would be possible without God's grace, blessings and faith which prevails all.

END

Prove Them Wrong

by Tonya Allgood, Esq.

I am often the only woman and minority in the room for meetings and court appearances. When I walk into court or meetings, I am often asked if I am in the right place or if my boss is on the way. I could never have imagined that such interactions would be a regular occurrence in my professional life. When I was growing up, my dream was to become a doctor so that I could have money – lots of it. But life has a funny way of pointing you in an entirely different direction than you've ever imagined for yourself. I have always loved a good debate. I am an avid reader and researcher. And I learned during my freshman year of biology at college that spurting bodily fluids and I did not get along.

So, I switched my career aspiration from doctor to lawyer because it aligned more with my talents (and would still allow me to make money – lots of it). I was going to be like Claire Huxtable but the new and improved version. When I decided to pursue law, I had never encountered a Black female attorney in real life. I had no idea where to start or what steps I would need to take to become a lawyer. So, I decided to discuss my goal with my undergraduate advisor.

I can't say for sure what my advisor knew about me when I approached her with my goal and my questions, other than that I was a young Black female. However, her response to me expressing my desire to become an attorney was that being a lawyer requires a lot of reading and might be out of my depth, and that perhaps I might want to pursue something less rigorous. In that moment, I recognized the attempt to demean and discourage me. I recognized the attempt to shatter my ambition, simply because I was who I was. Regrettably, this was not my first time encountering this sort of situation.

I have learned through various life experiences that achieving your career goals is not a linear process. There will be detours, discouragement, and struggle in every journey. There will be people who stand in your way and slam doors in your face because of the color of your skin, or because you are a woman, or because of both. These people, and the doors they slam in your face, are roadblocks. And what do we do when we encounter a roadblock? We don't stop – giving up because of temporary roadblocks is not an option. We find a way around it. We go over it. Under it. Around it.

I found a way around my undergraduate advisor. I got the information I needed, figured out the steps I needed to take, worked my behind off through law school prep and law school, and I graduated with honors from an amazing law school. This was a year long journey, and it was far from easy. But it taught me that investing in yourself through hard work and sacrifice to meet your goals is a truly satisfying experience. In addition, it reinforced for me that while others are entitled to their opinions of what you are capable or incapable of as a Black woman, those opinions are not controlling in your life.

During law school, I discovered that I loved contract law, specifically the federal contracting process. So, I decided I would take the bar exam and practice federal contract law as a Government attorney. Trying to break into this specialized area of the law as a newly minted Black female attorney was not a process for the faint of heart. My resume was rejected or not selected for an interview more times than I can count. In cases where I did get an interview, the interviews were demoralizing, to say the least. Every single interview panel was composed of middle-aged White males who seemed to be annoyed or in a rush, or both. Imagine trying to sell yourself to an interview panel that has obviously already written you off before the interview even started. Imagine sitting through interviews where the panel won't even make eye contact with you because they know they're not considering you despite how strong your experience, education, and credentials are. Not exactly encouraging.

Since I was running into roadblocks keeping me from being hired as a Government contracts attorney, I found another way to get my foot in the door. I knew I was more than qualified for a position as a Government contract specialist because I had a law degree. I applied for and was hired as a contract specialist intern. I worked as hard as I could in that position, and every chance I got I stepped up and took on assignments that would allow me to work with the contract attorneys. I showcased my knowledge and my work ethic to them every chance I got. I also made it known to them that I was licensed to practice law and interested in transitioning from a contract specialist to a contract attorney. I spoke what I wanted into existence, but also put in the work to get it.

When a position opened up in the legal office, I applied and was selected for an interview. My grasp of federal contracting principles, my hard work, and the value I added to the organization were undeniable. While I couldn't ultimately control who got the job, I put myself in the best position possible to be the strongest candidate. I got the contract attorney position and ran with it.

Once in the attorney position, I had to earn my title every single day. I was the only Black woman attorney in the office, and it was obvious that there were people waiting for me to fail. More precisely said, there were people actively rooting for me to fail. Some people even felt the need to let me know I was only in the position because of affirmative action or because "Obama was president." Again, I refused to let the opinions or intentions of others distract me. Their discomfort with my presence in the office was not my problem. I continued to work hard, and to learn as much as I could every single day. I let my work, and my results, speak for me. Even if my successes didn't change their minds about me, or Black women in general, they couldn't wish away my results and accomplishments.

Today, after about 12 years of practice, I am a GS-15 Senior Procurement Attorney for the Department of Defense, overseeing litigation of federal contract matters, and the award and administration of federal contracts. Getting to this point has been a journey with ups and downs, discouragement, frustration, and loss. But there has also been growth (both personal and professional), the achievement of career milestones, and the ever-present satisfaction of knowing that my work directly benefits and supports Warfighters and Armed Forces members doing amazing things for the country. Focusing on the positive helps to sustain me during the more trying times and situations.

One trying situation I regularly experience is walking into a courtroom or meeting where the shock, and sometimes disdain, of my presence is blatantly apparent. Based on my personal experience, I understand that there is a serious lack of representation of Black women attorneys in the field of Government contract law. I did not come across another Black female federal contract attorney until about 6 years into my career. In fact, today, more than 12 years into my career, I have only come across 3 other Black female federal contract attorneys. While the lack of representation of Black women in my specialized field of the law presents unique challenges, I see it as an opportunity. I have the opportunity to be a walking, talking example of what we, as Black women, are able to accomplish. I have the opportunity to share my knowledge and my testimony of overcoming discouragement and discrimination to achieve career goals others thought someone like me could never achieve.

Please understand that you will encounter roadblocks to your goals simply because you are a Black woman. Keep moving forward, regardless of whatever opposition you may be facing. Life can be tough...but so are you! Do not let the opinions of others define or limit you. PROVE. THEM. WRONG.

END

First Black Female Judge In The United States
Jane Matilda Bolin
Appointed 1962

WE RISE

Network = Net Worth

So often, people in general are misled into believing that networking means paying hundreds of dollars and having to book a flight to a big city in the United States for a conference with over five thousand other women who own businesses. Although large conference events can be extremely beneficial for an individual to network with others, it surely isn't the only way to connect with others. Think about how many Black women are business owners in America. That number should be so immense that having an exact number should be nearly impossible to calculate. Just imagine what would happen if we all came together and supported each other. Just economically speaking, Black women joining forces to support each other would transform the fashion, beauty supply, and entertainment industries economically forever. A prime example was recorded by WWD: *According to a report, Black women spent $7.5 billion per year on beauty products*. This is just one prime example of how essential it is that we recycle the money we spend within our own communities. (WWD, 2017) If we decided to have each other's back and support our fellow sisters, we would change the world we know forever.

You might be thinking, "How is it even possible to come together?" There is no one specific answer. For starters, a simple acknowledgment would be in order when you see another queen walking by at the grocery store or shopping mall. Instead of scrolling past her flyer for a business idea, reach out to her. Just a simple message saying "I support you" or "Keep pushing queen" can uplift a woman's spirits. There are so many businesses owned by Black women that it shouldn't be hard to support one of them whenever you can. *The American Express 2019 State of Women-Owned Businesses report has shown that there are 2,681,200 Businesses owned by Black women."*

Supporting one another creates the networking platform. The power of networking opens doors for you and the other person. "It's a small world" is very true, yet it's even smaller for Black women. We need to utilize resources out there. We as Black women have to keep in mind that it's not always what we know but essentially who we know. If we don't support each other first, who will? For queens who are aspiring to gain more clientele and expand their businesses, networking can be the spark your business needs. Sometimes it's not that Black women don't want to support you; they just might not know your business/organization exists.

We have so much to offer the world, so why reinvent thousands of wheels. We can just come together and work together to reach the common goal. The power of the dollar bill still is a deciding factor when it comes to the real change in society. So, once we start spending our money at each other's businesses, the greater our net worth will increase.

Networking equates to net worth. Stop thinking micro; elevate your strategy to macro. We spend the most money, we make others billionaires, yet we can count on one hand every Black woman billionaire in America. In order to have a net worth, you have to have a network. In today's world there are an abundance of avenues to network with others. Social media is one major way to network; we should take advantage of it. Networking can be done anywhere, from the grocery store to simply connecting with a person on social media. Networking is a tool Black woman in the past did not have and they still were resourceful. We as the Black women of today have to do our best to network with other women and men of all backgrounds, ages, races, and social class. Networking is the way the doors of opportunity are cracked open.

Build bridges, make connections and help the next woman as she aspires to do better for the next. Black women should knock down walls, not each other. *"We must love each other and support each other. We have nothing to lose but our chains." (Assata Shakur, 1987)* The key to understanding networking options is not limiting your audience and allowing yourself to connect with people you would not on average be connected with. The ways to make networking easy are simple, there are so many resources available to network with others you just have to be willing.

When in the phase of identifying networking groups, you must be willing to walk into a room and know that it is the perfect opportunity to sell yourself to others who are doing the same thing. The seed to make a change has been planted. So many platforms have been designed for this generation of Black women to work together. Some of which are Black Women Lead, Black Lives Matter, Black Girls Rock, Black Girl Magic just to name a few that amplified the voices of Black women and their underrepresented communities.

Tulsa Black business district burned in 1921, residents killed

Black Wall Street

Black Owned Block

Black Owned Product in Stock

Black Minds Came Together

Afrocentricity Working Around the Clock

Giving the Rest of The World Shell Shock

Opportunity Knocked

Blacks Snatched the Block

Turned the Lock

Began to Overstock

Up & Down the Sidewalk

Black People Invested in Stock

Kids on corners wearing smocks cleaning sidewalks

Not on the block slinging rock

Then Hate Gave A Knock

Burning Down Business on The Block

Leaving Blacks Dead on The Crosswalk

Black Wall Street Was on The Chopping Block

Dreams Shot on The Spot

Blood Streamed Down the Chalked Sidewalk

Blacks Building Better Burned Before Their Eyes

Poem by: Jasmine Poole

Ways To Elevate Your Network

- **Travel**
- **Be Consistent**
- **Invest In The Vision**
- **Support Others**
- **Master Time Management**
- **Utilize Social Media Platforms**
- **Always Have Business Cards On Hand**
- **Develop A Calendar To Attend Events & Promote Yourself/Brand**
- **Learn How To Describe Your Business/Brand In 2.5 Minutes or Less**
- **Build A Team That Can Market Your Brand In New Innovative Ways & Diverse Areas**

WE RISE

7

Togetherness

Picture a tree! Not just any tree but one that is strong and healthy and full of life. Now imagine us as Black women standing tall but not alone, because we have other trees beside us. Picture an entire forest of beautiful strong long trees who are all rooted in the same soil. The roots of these trees are intertwined with one another like hands joined with a voice. Black women stand up! Not just for yourselves! Stand up for your daughters, sisters, cousins, aunts and your ancestors. We have proven time and time again that we struggle but our strength outweighs even our storms. We are like trees that grow better together, and through all of the storms and rain, we use it to help us better ourselves and improve. All that we as a race have been through hasn't done anything except bring forth even more awareness. The pain and scars are the badges that we should never be ashamed of; it is the overcoming that makes it a testimony and no longer a test. Together we share struggles we can truly understand. The pain of our past and some of the pain of your present use these women as proof that you will rise.

Not all women can say their ancestors endured 400 years of slavery and countless decades of never having a voice to make their own decisions in the country. For many of us we have just been living our own lives and suffering in silence. This book has been not just the stories of Black women of all ages and backgrounds. Not one of us is the same despite what the world tries to attest. Some of us are teachers, doctors, nurses, lawyers, construction workers, engineers, pastors, politicians, judges, police officers, psychologists, therapists, and authors. Together we rise.

We rise in the roles we have in our lives as mothers, daughters, sisters, grandmothers, wives, girlfriends, single-mothers, widows, and most of all Black women. We rise to the challenges the world throws our way each day in our individual lives. We no longer choose to stay in the place that might feel comfortable but instead come together and rise once and for all.

There has always been strength in numbers. We can rise above anything with God, but he gave us each other to hold one another up.

We Rise for Harriet Tubman, Sojourner Truth, Ella Baker, Coretta Scott King, Maya Angelou, Assata Shakur and countless more. God gave us the strength to rise.

That one in a million

Jasmine E. Poole

Emergency delivery! It was time to make my grand entrance into this world. It was following a nearly fatal car accident for me and my pregnant mother at the time. My mother was only six months pregnant with me when I took my first breath after being rushed to the hospital. Doctors said I was dangerously premature. They also went on to explain how abnormal of a case this was. The medical physicians advised my mom to start praying because the chances were slim for her newborn baby to survive. My mother was faced with the scary reality that if her baby was to pull through that it would never walk, talk, or live a normal life. All that my mother heard was that her child won't be "normal" due to the accident and the damage it did to her. "We are very sorry, but your daughter will suffer from auditory processing disorder", so she will have a learning disability that will limit her. So, reading, writing, or even speaking might be impossible, the doctors said, "This child has a one in a million chance of beating the odds against her".

Overcoming Elementary School

Every year of my childhood, I spent my birthday in my least favorite place in the world. September 7th was the first day of school. "Oh joy" was all I sarcastically would say as I got on the school bus every year. For the first three years of elementary school, I just coasted on by. It was smooth sailing from first grade to the third grade; smooth all the way up until the day my third-grade teacher called on me to read out loud to the rest of the class. All I remember was staring down at a page of tiny words, and after every second that passed my heartbeat got faster and faster. Frantically! I raised my hand and said I have to use the bathroom. My teacher at the time insisted I take the hall pass and walk down to the lavatory. Once I made it to the bathroom, I began to hyperventilate in the stall and cry. Up until that day, I never had been asked to read aloud. Little did I know, this was only the beginning of a long road ahead.

So as the weeks passed, I managed to maneuver my way to the nurse's office, bathroom or water fountain when it was my turn to read. I mastered getting out of reading; I had it down to a science. Whenever it was time to read as a class, I would count the classmates whose turn it was to read before mine. As soon as it reached the second or third person before me, I would throw up my hand. It took months before the teacher picked up on my slick strategy. After connecting the dots, my teacher sent a letter home, and I knew letters home meant trouble, so I trashed it. That bought me a few more days of time to come up with an excuse. I knew I had to think fast. When my teacher finally tried calling my house, I was so happy because the house phone had been off for months. I just knew I got away with whatever trouble I was in, until a group of ladies in fancy business suits sat silently behind me for an entire day typing on their laptops and scribbling notes. So many thoughts raced in and out of my mind as to why they were here and what they wanted with me. Towards the end of the day during recess, I remember being called down to the counseling office. I walked in, and my heart dropped to the floor. There sitting at a long conference table was my mom and dad and those two women in suits from earlier. All I could think was, "I am in big trouble if my mom and my dad had to leave work to come up to my school".

After standing frozen and speechless for what felt like forever, I heard a voice say, "Hi Jasmine. We are the child study team case managers, have a seat sweetheart" it was my teacher, "Do you know why you are here?" I said "Yes I think so" as I looked up at both my parents. A few short moments later one of the women wrote on an eraser board the words "cat" "dog" "happy" "sad" and "mad". Can you read each of these words out loud for us sweetie?" the woman in the fancy suit said. So, I looked up at my mom, and she smiled warmly. I took a glance at my dad, and he gave me a look of reassurance; he knew I could read the words. So, I read all the words slowly and once I did my dad said you see nothing wrong with her.

I began to get scared as I noticed the lady pull out a book for me to read out loud. I felt my heart begin to beat really fast, and my palms begin to sweat. Then suddenly, "Jasmine read from the red arrow down to the bottom arrow." It took all I had to not get up and leave like I was so accustomed to. I gave it all I had, and I wasn't able to read the paragraph without assistance on every other word. Tears began to pile up behind my eyelids, and it made all the words blurry; tears began to hit the page, and I balled up my fist in anger and embarrassment. The whole room got silent, and my teacher said, "It's okay Jasmine, it's okay". My teacher said are you ready to go back to recess with the class and I shook my head yes and let out a sigh of relief.

Being switched over to remedial class was one of the most humiliating and demoralizing hurdles I have ever had to face. I was always the funny and well-mannered kid who didn't give off the small bus stereotype appearance. I wasn't neglected at home like the majority of my classmates who you could tell just by looking at them that they hadn't bathed in weeks. While the other half were in there because of their behavioral issues. Those often were the ones that lived in drug houses and prided themselves on the guns and gangs they were around at home. My hair and hygiene stayed fresh, and I took pride in the newest athletic knock off gear I could get my hands on. I grew up in a Christian home and went to church every day of the week besides Friday nights. Growing up in a two-parent household and being the middle child out of three was sometimes a blessing or a curse. I lived in the suburbs but with a below poverty lifestyle just to survive. Having the newest sneakers wasn't the case for me. I still remember getting one pair of White and Black K-Swiss tennis shoes before school started in September every year. By October, my shoes would be so ragged and worn I would pack a Black sharpie just to shade in the light spots. I would have holes on the soles of my sneakers sometimes so I would wear two pairs of socks and watch out for puddles. I knew from a very early age that sacrifice was critical in order to provide for your loved ones. My mom worked a lot, and my dad was on disability after being diagnosed with bipolar mental disorder. School wasn't my priority growing up, and it certainly was not the highlight of my day.

After my first year of elementary, I was labeled with an Individualized Education Program (IEP) and tossed in remedial support classes, commonly known as "special education" or "slow class". I was assigned a case manager in the child study team office who I would meet with twice a year for evaluations. The case manager in the child study team said to me after every meeting that I was never going to be able to get placed in regular education classes. She advised me to keep doing my best at the level I was placed at.

I recall always hearing teachers say, "step aside and make room for the special ed students coming down the hall". That was pure embarrassment. More than half of the school knew who I was and that I wasn't like those other kids in Special Ed classes. The "normal kids" would whisper things like, "YOOOO LOOK AT JAS; SHE IN THE RETARD CLASS", while others would laugh and tap each other and point. That humiliation followed me all the way through my early years of school, so as a result, I became very angry and started to leave class and spend most of my time in the bathroom washing my hands for hours it seemed. I hated lunch time and anytime the whole class of all 10 students had to be seen walking to Library, Art, Music, or even my favorite Gym class. I would pull the top neck part of my t-shirt to try to cover my face of shame. I would even try to stand in the back of the line and drag behind walking as slow as I could to create a gap between me and the next person in line.

Special Ed wasn't that bad when it was just us all in the same class with the class door closed. Those were some of the best moments. A lot of us were in there because we learned slower than most or dealt with behavior issues. So, the class was filled with the "baddest students" in the whole school. The school knew the right person to put in that class. She was someone who would love us just the way we were and do her best to teach us and help guide us; her name was Ms. Johnson. If it had not been for Ms. Johnson, I don't know if I would have ever wanted to become an educator. Being a young ten-year-old Black girl and having a teacher that looks like you triggered something in me. Ms. Johnson was the first teacher to ever show me she cared about me and the first to not treat me like I was illiterate but instead like a "normal kid". As elementary school was coming to an end, I knew I didn't want to leave my comfort zone.

Middle School

Ever since the first day I stepped foot in middle school, I knew I had to put up my guard and protect myself from all the shame and humiliation that lurked. Middle school was a whole new ball game. I began to notice how girls started dressing differently and their bodies, unlike mine, had gotten womanlier. I was still the flat chested tomboy who everybody would get confused with a boy during gym class when teams were being picked. I still remember the gym teacher telling one of the kids during gym class to pick one girl and one boy, "I'll pick the girl with the pink shorts and the boy with the jersey and braids". Let's just say I loved Allen Iverson. Wearing basketball jerseys and my hair braided in cornrows straight back was my signature style back then. Even though this was what I chose to wear because my mother and father never forced me to wear girly clothes, it still hurt my feelings being called tomboy, ugly, boy, roughneck, and the worst of all, manly. Over time in middle school, I grew thicker skin and even though I still got talked about behind my back, nobody said anything to my face. I began to fight a lot of the boys in the neighborhood, and they began to respect me and leave me alone. Instead of making fun of me, they would invite me to play sports with them outside after school. So, a lot of the girls labeled me one of the guys and would talk about me and make me feel like I was the ugliest girl in the world. It has been said that middle school girls are the meanest people on earth, and I certainly agree with that statement.

While most girls my age back then would wear the tightest jeans possible and an extra small t-shirt and put on as much makeup as possible all to just sit at the basketball courts and watch the boys play, I was the girl with a t-shirt and baggy basketball shorts on with two braids going back playing basketball or football with the boys.

It wasn't until my 8th grade year in middle school, I had my first crush, and being that I was still in special education classes with all of the kids who had behavioral issues, I would strategize to dart out the class before the boy I had a crush on would see me leaving the special class. This worked for a short time only. Then one day, I left to go to the bathroom, and he was in the hallways; it was too late to turn back around. So, I had to face the humiliation. Let's just say he and I still continued to have a crush on each other and pass notes each period after the bell would ring. What was happening to me was that all of a sudden, I wanted to wear jeans like the other girls and try to tame my natural hair to be straight like all the other girls. Back then, relaxers were used frequently in the Black community, and women would always say how beautiful I would be if only my hair wasn't nappy. So, after noticing all the girls in school with straight hair, I wanted to shake the tomboy image once and for all, so I begged my mom to let me get a relaxer. That was the turning point of my life from little girl to young woman. Still battling with being one of the cool kids and having to hide the fact that I was in remedial classes, I began to devote most of my class time to making others laugh and enjoy the spotlight being the class clown. I never did horrible in school, but I surely wasn't the Honor Roll student. My middle school case manager often advised me to attend tutoring after school to help me with my reading skills. I always declined the offer and rushed straight home to go outside and play. I hated school, so why would I want to stay after for more school. Besides gym and lunch, my favorite time of the day was seeing the school buses line up in front of the school before dismissal.

Until one day, my gym teacher asked me to play on the school co-ed basketball team. I hated basketball the most out of every sport growing up, because it had so many rules, I thought. The gym teacher said every team needed one girl on the team. He also encouraged me to give it a chance. So, I stayed after school and decided to give it a shot. All the boys wanted me as their only girl on the team because they knew I was the most athletic girl in the school. So, I was selected to be on the team "Temple" all the teams were named after colleges. I will never forget that first game, down by two and one of the boys inbounded the ball to me; I was supposed to pass it back, but I took the shot instead and everyone on my team screamed "NOOOOOO" and sure enough it was a SWISH! Instantly, all the boys on my team came rushing towards me hugging me and hitting me on the back with excitement. That was the day I found my purpose! The looks on all those faces when I made that shot and the excitement and pride I felt inside. That was one of the greatest moments of my life. The moment I fell in love with basketball, I will forever cherish. After that day, I couldn't put the basketball down. I slept beside it in my bed. I even took it to school. Sometimes, I would forget my backpack, but I never forgot my basketball. Not a day went by after I made that shot that I didn't go practice at the basketball courts. Before being allowed to go to the basketball courts, I would shoot the ball and aim to hit the top of the shed house in my backyard. I would pretend I made the shot and close my eyes and picture an arena of people cheering my name. I finally found something positive and something I wanted to be remembered for. When determination struck, there was no stopping me. A normal day for me was getting up before school at 5:00 am, running one mile around my neighborhood with my basketball, going home, taking a shower and making the school bus. After school, I began going to tutoring and getting my grades up. After tutoring, I would rush home and shoot 1,000 jump shots and force myself to stay until I shot all 1,000. Even in the snow, I would bring a shovel to the courts and section off spots to shoot from. I even went as far as playing in the freezing rain. I was determined to make it; and I was proving it to everyone, including the doctors who said I would never walk or run that anything is possible as long as you keep God first and work hard.

High School

Freshman year of high school, I was in for a rude awakening. I was now the new kid on the block and the name I made for myself in middle school was no longer relevant. I found myself the little fish in the ocean. Tryouts that year had forty plus girls fighting to make the team. The head coach knew I was the star at the middle school, but he wanted to see me play against seniors and juniors. I never backed down from any challenges so why start now, is all I could think. So, after going head to head with the best upperclassmen I gained some respect from them. The only problem was my academics; I never was the school type, but the high school coach made it clear grades come before athletics, so if I planned on playing basketball at the varsity level, I had to do well in school. That was my turning point academically. I decided to get a tutor after school and sit in the front of my classes and prove that I didn't belong in these classes anymore and that I was capable of being in "normal classes." After having earned Honor Roll my entire freshman year of high school, I was blessed to be removed from special education classes and be with the "normal kids." That was one of the happiest moments of my life. I no longer had to be late to class on purpose just because I was walking with my teammates down the hall and didn't want them to see the class I'm going into or sitting in the back of the classroom just so that students walking by won't see me and laugh. Finally, I thought I made it to my truth, but all along I didn't embrace who I was the whole time. I found myself still trying to impress everyone and prove to people that I wasn't stupid, and I was pretty and that I was one of the greatest basketball players.

High School was some of the greatest childhood memories I have to cherish, not only did I become one of the hardest working and superior female basketball players of all time in school history I also found a love for school politics and ran for office and became class president my sophomore year. I began to notice I had leadership qualities and loved making a difference especially for the people who were still in those classes like I was. Out of nowhere a traumatic knee injury came crashing down breaking my right patella tendon, leaving me scared, angry and confused about what to do. I thought my basketball career was over forever, and I was asking God why he would let this happen to me after I worked so hard to stop fighting and getting in trouble and instead become an honor roll student athlete.

This was my senior year. I thought it was gonna be a fairytale like my favorite movie at the time "Love and Basketball", but instead, it was a nightmare; colleges started sending my calls to voicemail, and letters stopped coming in. At this point all I had was God, family, and education. I learned in that moment that athletes can come and go but academics will forever be. During that dark time in my life, I decided to start a youth outreach program at seventeen years old to help kids in my neighborhood with their academic success. I had no clue this would be my calling. On June 15, 2013 I got called down for the last child study meeting to confirm my exit out of high school. My case manager at the time assigned to me was a woman who barely knew my name and hardly ever looked up from her fancy laptop to see how I was doing. Her last words to me were, "So Ms. Poole, what are your plans for after high school?" I responded swiftly and so excited "College". She responded so sarcastically, "You? College? Sweetie, college is hard and it's not for everyone, it's still not too late for me to find you a job or a trade school". At that exact moment there I was again being told how I could never be a college student. I got up from the chair I sat in and said thank you for your time and proceeded out of her office, never to see that woman again.

College

There was one coach who offered me an athletic scholarship to play for her Division II women's basketball team. At that moment, I knew God had not given up on me or turned his back on my life. I knew in my heart that with just one chance I would give it my all both in the classroom and on the basketball court. So, that is exactly what I did. If I wasn't in the library, I was in the gym, waking up at 4:00 am just to be in the gym at 5:00am then study sweaty in the library before class. This was my daily routine and it earned me the Dean's List and accompanying it was my 3.9 GPA I earned in my first college year. No matter what I did academically, I still always felt like that same, Special Ed tomboy in the back of the class with her head down, until the day I received an email stating that a College wanted me to play basketball at their college on an academic scholarship. All I could think was academic scholarship, who wants me to be at their college on an academic scholarship? This was mind blowing to me. Needless to say, I agreed and went on to continue my studies and play basketball at a college after graduating with my associate degree at the junior college.

I still remember waiting in the academic office at my soon-to-be new college. It was the middle of June, and I was thrilled and nervous to be sitting at one of the most prestigious all girls' Catholic schools remaining in the United States. The secretary said, "I may come back now to see your advisor." So, nervously I got up out of the chair in the waiting room and proceeded toward the office door cracked open. The slim White woman at her desk with lots of gray hair said, "Come on in Jasmine and have a seat." I was shocked she knew my name. I always get just another number, but for the first time it doesn't seem that way. The woman said to me. "Have you chosen a major of study yet?" I responded by saying "No". Then she said, "Well we can take care of that right now, what do you wish to study?" I said, "I don't

227

know." I started to say I only came here to play basketball but the reason I was truly there was because of my academic scholarship. So, I said, "Maybe a teacher." The women responded with excitement saying, "Yes, we have one of the best education programs in the state." So, she began to scroll down the list of subject areas I could study to teach someday. She said, "Would you like to be a math or science teacher?" I responded back with a fast "Noooo". Next, she moved on to ask if I would like to teach history of English. I said yes, maybe History but definitely not English. I knew English was out of the question; anything but English. I always struggled with words, reading, and anything remotely close to the two, so I knew English was out of the question. So, I chose history and after signing off on my schedule for the incoming semester I was good to go, well so I thought.

After the first week of classes, I found myself miserable and feeling purposeless. So, I prayed and asked God to direct my path and surely two days later I received an email stating that the academic advisor needed to see me. So, when I entered her office, she said that the English department was seeking more students and that this major would be broader and help with a wider range of internships and careers after college. So, I knew this was a sign and I always stand on God's promises and in his word, he said he would never leave or forsake me. So, I knew that becoming an English major student wouldn't break me but make me into a better student and child of God. So long behold the same little girl who couldn't read fluently until the age of 12 years old turned into the same young woman a few years later who went to college and became an English major in one of the most historic colleges in all of the state of New Jersey.

That one in a million

After overcoming adversity time and time again, I decided to be the person I needed growing up, starting with empowering youth who are constantly told that they are not capable. That is what inspired me to start my own nonprofit organization Jesus People Elite Enterprise (JPELITE). Growing up, I was friends with the kid in the wheelchair and the star athlete. Some of my closest groups of friends were ranked the highest academically in the school, while the other half were oftentimes flunking classes or even dropping out of school. God blessed me with a personality that can relate to all kinds of people which became one of my strongest strengths. Having friends who could help me study to pass statistics was important, but also having friends that could walk me home from school at night without getting jumped was equally important. I was blessed to be able to relate with both. Now as a community leader those same strengths reveal themselves whenever I have a meeting with a pastor of a church, or a conversation with a drug dealer on the streets. God made it possible for me to be on both levels without having to fake it; I just stay true to myself and live in my truth.

Living in your truth just means being comfortable in your own skin while fulfilling the purpose God has over your life. Did I ever imagine as a little Black girl who struggled in school to overcome being picked on for being in special education classes that I would one day graduate from college with a bachelor's degree with the Highest Honors English Degree, having made the Dean's list all four semesters? Who would have guessed that the little Black girl with the braids and baggy jersey on, who cut class because she couldn't read, would become a college graduate with a bachelor's degree in English and would work towards becoming an English teacher to teach students with disabilities like she once had? And that same little girl would go on to attend graduate school at one of the top universities in the state of New Jersey to receive a master's degree in Public Administration, with the hopes of furthering her studies to receive a Community Development PhD to someday fulfill the vision God put inside of her to open a community center? Now finally after having played basketball on nearly every level possible, she hangs up her jersey to pick up a coaches board. She is the head girls basketball coach for her hometown high school and is the founder and director of the very first girls basketball feeder program in her town's history.

As I was once that little girl, I must say God has used me in ways I would have never imagined. I stand firm on his promise that in Phillipians 4:13 "I can do all things through Christ that strengthens me". When I was born the doctors said I had a one in a million chance of overcoming the odds, I'm living proof that God made me *"That one in a million"*.

"God opened the door for me, so I just want to hold the door open for others."

Jasmine Poole, Author

Acknowledgements

God, in His almighty wisdom, has allowed me yet another opportunity to put on paper the voices that often get pushed aside. I am eternally grateful for each of the beautiful, brilliant, and brave Black women who shared glimpses of their life stories. I'm grateful to Nathan Lee Gadsden who always had a ready ear and comforting shoulder when writing this book became exhausting for me. It is because of his literary expertise that each of our voices became adequately conveyed. A spiritual thank you to all of the prayer warriors. So many times, when I have not had the strength to continue, it was your prayers that gave me the endurance to keep going. I thank each wonderful woman who left a part of themselves on each of these pages. Your legacy is a blessing for every future generation. Finally, many thanks to every Black woman who came before us. May we learn from your sacrifices how to rise together so that we may be guided towards wisdom and love.

Jasmine Poole

Bibliography

Abernethy, A. (2020). Fuller Studio.

https://fullerstudio.fuller.edu/womens-leadership-in-the-african-american-church.

About Teen Pregnancy. (2017). Centers for Disease Control and Prevention.

https://www.cdc.gov/teenpregnancy/about/index.htm.

Angelou, M. (2013). Mom & Me & Mom. New York: Random House.

Barnes, Z. (2017). SELF.

https://www.self.com/story/Black-women-health-conditions.

Barnes, Z. (2020). SELF.

https://www.self.com/contributor/zahra-barnes.

Black Women & Sexual Violence. African American women on a political, economic, and cultural level.

https://now.org/wp-content/uploads/2018/02/Black-Women-and-Sexual-Violence-6.pdf.

Dallard, S. (1990). Ella Baker: A Leader Behind the Scenes. Indianapolis: Silver Burdett Press.

Depression in Black Women. Black Women's Health Imperative.

https://bwhi.org/2017/07/31/depression-Black-women-know-youre-depressed

Du Bios, W. E. B. (1903). The Souls of Black Folk. Chicago: A. G. McClurg.

Duffin, E. (2020). Statistica.

https://www.statista.com/statistics/205106/number-of-Black-families-with-a-female-householder-in-the-us.

Focusing on Black Women's Health. (2020). Nurturing You Women's Health & Wellness

> https://www.nurturingyou.com/focusing-on-Black-womens-health.

Garvey, M. (1935). The Tragedy of White Injustice, Third Edition. London: [publisher not identified].

Kaliszewski, M. (2020). *Understanding Substance Abuse Among African Americans.* American Addiction Centers.

> https://americanaddictioncenters.org/rehab-guide/addiction-statistics/african-americans.

Kendall, J. (1995). Lady in Waiting: Becoming God's Best While Waiting for Mr. Right. United Kingdom: Hatchette.

Lester, J. (2005). Day of Tears. New York: Hyperion.

Li, W. (2019). Eat to Beat Disease. New York: Grand central Publishing.

Literacy as Freedom. (2014). SAAM Smithsonian American Art Museum.

> (https://americanexperience.si.edu/wp-content/uploads/2014/09/Literacy-as-Freedom.pdf).

McFadden, B. (2001). The Warmest December. Brooklyn, N.Y.: Akashic Books.

McNair, J. (2000). Barbara Jordan Journey to Freedom.

Neal-Barnett, A. (2018). *To Be Female, Anxious and Black.* Anxiety and Depression Association of America.

> https://adaa.org/learn-from-us/from-the-experts/blog-posts/consumer/be-female-anxious-and-Black.

Sanchez, S. (1984). Homegirls And Handgrenades. Buffalo, N.Y.: White Wine Press.

Scott King, C. (2017). My Life, My Love, My Legacy. New York: Henry Holt and Company, Inc.

Shakur, A. (1987). Assata: An Autobiography. Chicago: Chicago Review Press, Inc.

Shakur, T. (1999). The Rose That Grew from Concrete. New York: Simon & Schuster.

Spinale, L. (1999). Sojourner Truth. North Mankato, Minn.: The Child's World.

Sterling, D. (1954). Freedom Train: The Story of Harriet Tubman. New York: Scholastic Books.

Taylor, E. (2020). *Little Known Black History*. Black americaweb.com. https://Blackamericaweb.com/2013/12/23/little-known-Black-history-fact-spelman-college/

Violet Botanical Skincare. (2017). African American Women and The Coast of Beauty. https://www.violetbody.net/blogs/news/african-american-women-and-the-cost-of-beauty.

Welch, C. (2000). Ida B. Wells-Barnett: Powerhouse with a Pen. Minneapolis: Carolrhoda Books.

Kentz, Nikki. (2020). Black Women Are the Most Educated Group in The U.S. https://www.thoughtco.com/Black-women-most-educated-group-us-4048763.

CPSIA information can be obtained
at www.ICGtesting.com
Printed in the USA
LVHW082325200821
695735LV00003B/78